THE LOWFAT GRILL

*175 Surprisingly Succulent
Recipes for Meats, Marinades,
Vegetables, Sauces, and More!*

DONNA RODNITZKY

PRIMA
PUBLISHING

Prima Publishing and colophon are trademarks
of Prima Communications, Inc.

Illustrations by Richard Sheppard

Library of Congress Cataloging-in-Publication Data

Rodnitzky, Donna.
The lowfat grill : 175 surprisingly succulent recipes for meats, marinades, vegetables, sauces, and more / by Donna Rodnitzky.
p.   cm.
Includes index.
ISBN 0-7615-0265-3
1. Barbecue cookery.   2. Low-fat diet–Recipes.
I. Title.
TX840.B3R62   1995

641.5'784–dc20   95-33234
                                                                                        CIP

96 97 98 99 DD 10 9 8 7 6 5 4 3
Printed in the United States of America

HOW TO ORDER

Single copies of this book may be ordered from Prima Publishing, P.O. Box 1260BK, Rocklin, CA 95677, telephone (916) 632-4400. Quantity discounts are also available. On your letterhead, include information concerning the intended use of the books and the number of books you wish to purchase.

CONTENTS

PREFACE

THIS COOKBOOK IS ABOUT THE JOY OF INDULGING IN healthful cuisine that is delicious yet light and low in fat. It seems as though all the foods many of us enjoyed most when growing up were slathered with butter or deep-fried in cooking oil or shortening, but times have changed. Now that we understand more about healthful dining and appreciate the importance of limiting our fat intake, these mouth-watering morsels have become mere memories. Too often we are faced with the sad fact that the foods that taste best and rekindle the fondest memories are least healthful—and what better example of this dilemma than those wonderful meals prepared on an outdoor grill.

Whether a family picnic or a day at the beach with friends, who doesn't have a Pavlovian response to the memory of steaks or plump hamburgers sizzling on a barbecue grill, engulfed in an aromatic haze of charcoal smoke? As good as they taste, too many of these grilled treats contain more fat than is acceptable for a modern healthful diet. Does that mean we have to abandon this culinary tradition? Absolutely not! This book tells you how to limit the fat content of grilled foods while enhancing their natural flavors and preserving the smoky taste that is unique to grilling.

Let me explain how I met this challenge. My family and I realized that many grilled foods contain too much fat, but we didn't want to give up the wonderful ritual and taste of grilling. Grilling is not only a way of imparting a unique taste to foods, it is a happening–an escape from the kitchen and an opportunity to commune with nature (if only on the back porch or patio). For us, it was a family tradition. I had my marching orders. After much experimentation, I discovered the secret to tasty lowfat grilling.

You will be pleasantly surprised, as I was, that the marinades I developed for the leaner cuts of meat not only enhanced their flavor but tenderized them as well. Lean turkey is transformed into delicious turkey teriyaki, chicken breasts brim with the zestiness of lemon and pepper, and lean cuts of beef and vegetables combine in a grill-top wok to become a wonderful stir-fry. The smoky flavor from the grill mingling with the right spices, herbs, and sauces combine to make the simplest cut of meat a lowfat gourmet treat.

It is common knowledge that leaner cuts of meat are often less tender and less tasty and therefore not ideal for grilling. This cookbook, with its tenderizing and flavor-enhancing techniques, will allow you to use these less fatty cuts. Here are the lean cuts of meat you should choose for lowfat grilling:

Lean Cuts of Meat for Grilling

Beef	Pork	Lamb	Veal
round tip	tenderloin	loin chop	cutlet
top round	boneless top loin chop	leg	loin chop
eye of round	boneless ham, cured		
tenderloin	center loin of chop		
sirloin			

A useful rule of thumb is that the words "round" and "loin" signify lean beef and "loin" or "leg" imply lean pork. USDA "Select" beef is the leanest or has the least amount of marbling (these are the flecks of fat found within the meat), and "choice" is the second leanest. Keep in mind that these lean cuts of meat can be made even leaner by up to 50% just by removing any visible fat before cooking.

Grilling is also an ideal way to prepare seafood, and this book is full of recipes featuring a wide variety of ocean bounty. Just as with meats, combining seafood with the right seasoned vegetables and utilizing a flavorful marinade before grilling or a zesty sauce afterward results in a wonderful lowfat taste sensation that will satisfy the most demanding gourmet.

The majority of the recipes in the cookbook were tested on a kettle grill. However, most of the recipes can be adapted to a gas grill or almost any other type of grill. Depending on the heat and efficiency of your grill, cooking time may vary. Whatever technique, grill, or family secret you may possess for the perfect barbecue, this book will introduce you to an exciting new way to enjoy lighter cooking. Most of the recipes in this book can be started a day ahead and are quick and easy to prepare. A trip to an Asian food store will allow you to stock up on unique ingredients, and of course, substitutions are always possible. In fact, that is the beauty of these recipes. Just like chemistry, by combining a few key ingredients you can create a marvelous marinade that will allow the flavor in foods to come alive with a piquancy and zest that will surprise and please your family and guests.

I invite you to experience a world of wonderful flavors and to enjoy a more healthful lifestyle.

ACKNOWLEDGMENTS

This book would not have been possible without the cooperation and support of Prima Publishing. I would like to thank Acquisitions Editor, Alice Anderson; Project Editor, Susan Silva; Senior Project Editor, Steven Martin; Lindy Dunlavey, cover designer; and Bunny Martin, food stylist, for their efficiency and professionalism in guiding this book toward publication.

A special thank you goes to my husband, Bob, and my three children, David, Adam, and Laura who gave me their enthusiastic encouragement and support. Most of all, I appreciate their willingness to taste most of the recipes.

HELPFUL GUIDELINES

A WIDE VARIETY OF GRILLS IS AVAILABLE, EACH WITH unique characteristics. Some of the recipes in this cookbook were tested on a Weber Charcoal Kettle grill and others on a gas grill, but good results can be obtained with any of the popular grills described here.

GRILLS

Kettle grills

The kettle grill's hood and base are rounded so that heat is evenly reflected off of all surfaces and back onto the food. This makes cooking time shorter and locks in the natural flavors and juices of foods. Although the hood is removable, it is usually advisable to cook with it on. This limits the oxygen supply and prevents flare-ups, eliminating the need for water bottles and reducing the possibility of burning the food. Regulation of heat is controlled by vents on the base and hood, which should be in the open position when starting the charcoal and while cooking. However, if the heat from the coals becomes too great, the vents on the base can be closed. Make sure to use insulated barbecue mitts when adjusting the vents because they will be hot to the touch. Lastly, when the coals are cool, it is necessary to remove all accumulated ashes from the vents at the bottom of the grill to allow for proper ventilation with your next use.

Braziers or open grills

The open grill is most often made without a hood. It is round in shape, has a single cooking rack, and is supported on long legs. Some models are made with a half hood or wind screen. The brazier is an inexpensive way to grill, but its use should be limited to those foods that do not take a long time to prepare because the coals burn down to ashes very quickly. With this type of grill, it is useful to keep a water bottle nearby to extinguish any flare-ups that may occur when fat drips onto the coals.

Hooded grills

Hooded grills resemble kettle grills except they are square or rectangular and the hood is hinged onto the base. Food can be cooked either with the hood open as on a brazier or with it closed, allowing more smoke to accumulate and generating greater heat so that the food cooks faster.

Smoker

A smoker is an elongated, cylindrical grill. In addition to a fuel grate and a cooking rack, a pan is positioned between them. Water is added to this pan and when the liquid gets hot, it produces steam. Soaked, smoking wood chips of your choice are sprinkled on top of the hot coals. The combination of the steam from the hot water, cooking the food at a very low temperature, and smoke from the wood chips allows the food to acquire a very intense smoky flavor and at the same time remain moist and juicy. It may be necessary to add additional coals every 50 to 60 minutes, but avoid opening the lid unnecessarily as it may add to the cooking time.

Gas and electric grills

Gas and electric grills are very similar in design to a kettle or hooded grill. However, they use permanent lava rocks or ceramic briquette-shaped rocks instead of charcoal. These rocks are heated by an underlying gas burner or electric heating element. The major advantage of these grills is that they get hot quickly, and the briquettes do not have to be replaced since they do not burn down to ashes. A gas grill requires a gas canister or a natural gas hook-up; an electric grill requires a nearby electrical outlet. Both of these grills impart a smoky flavor when drippings from the food fall onto the hot briquettes and vaporize; however, the flavors are not nearly as intense as when charcoal is used.

LIGHTING COALS

When using a grill that requires charcoal, it is important to get all of the briquettes equally hot so that the food is uniformly cooked. The best way to accomplish this is to stack 20 to 30 coals in a pyramid before starting them on fire. There are several effective techniques to start the coals or fire as discussed below. After burning for 25 to 30 minutes, the coals should all be ashen gray on the outside and within the pyramid there should be a red glow. Using barbecue tongs, spread the coals out so they cover an area a little wider than the food to be cooked.

FIRE STARTERS

Chimney starter

The chimney is used to get coals hot in a short period of time. It is a metal cylinder with holes on the sides to allow for ventilation. It may have a wooden handle. The best way to use the chimney is to place some crumbled newspaper on the bottom of it and place coals on top. Open all the vents and set fire to the newspaper. In a very short time, the coals will be hot. Using the handle on the chimney, transfer the hot coals onto the fuel grate. If the chimney does not have a handle, be certain to use insulated barbecue mitts to transfer the hot coals.

Kindling
Take pieces of newspaper and roll them diagonally into a long, narrow cylinder. Grasp the ends and tie them into a knot. Place the knots in the bottom of the fuel grate and cover them with pieces of dry twigs or wood scraps. Loosely mound six to seven coals on top of the pile. Carefully ignite the newspaper knots. As coals ignite, add more coals to the mound, continuing this process until all the coals have been added. Using tongs, carefully spread out the coals over the fuel grate once they have become hot.

Electric starter
The electric starter consists of a heating element attached to an extended handle with a cord that plugs into an electrical outlet. The element is placed among the coals and when it is plugged in, it gets hot enough to ignite the coals resting on it. The hot coals ignite the others and, in time, all of the coals will become hot.

Block starters
Two to three of these small chemically treated cubes are placed among the coals and ignited with a match. They do not affect the taste of the food and are very easy to use.

Liquid starters
Liquid starters are a popular way to light coals. However, the chemicals in the starter are absorbed by the coals and can impart an unpleasant taste to your

food. The best way to avoid this potential problem is to place only a few coals on the fuel grate and sprinkle them with starter. Add the remaining coals and ignite the treated coals. Using this technique, the majority of the coals are untreated and cannot generate a chemical taste. Never add additional starter if any of the coals are still burning as this practice is a serious fire hazard.

BRIQUETS AND WOOD CHIPS

Charcoal briquettes

Charcoal briquettes are made of carbonized scraps of wood, combined with a filler and compressed into the shape of a briquette. Often, chemicals are added that allow the coals to light more quickly. However, food cooked over these coals containing these additives can have an unpleasant taste. To minimize this problem, make sure all of the coals are uniformly ashen gray which indicates that the chemicals have completely burned away and are no longer a source of fumes.

Hardwood charcoal

Hardwood charcoal is made of wood without the addition of fillers or chemical additives, and therefore, does not give an unpleasant taste to grilled food. It burns hotter than ordinary charcoal briquettes. Charcoal of this type is frequently made of hickory, maple, oak, cherry, or mesquite.

Smoking chips or chunks

Smoking chips or chunks are used to impart a unique flavor to the food more so than to act as a fuel. They may be made of woods such as mesquite, cherry, alder, maple, hickory, oak, walnut, or apple, each having its own distinctive smoke aroma and flavor. Wood chips or chunks will generate the most smoke when allowed to sit in water for at least 30 minutes before they are scattered onto the hot coals. If you have any grape vines, they can also be used in the same way.

ACCESSORIES

There is no end to the number of accessories that have added new dimensions to creative grilling and at the same time, have made it so easy! All of the accessories described here or mentioned in the recipes are inexpensive; becoming a fully equipped grilling chef is relatively easy. On the other hand, you may find that with a little improvisation, cooking utensils you already own can be used for the same purpose.

Wire brush
This is an essential tool for keeping the grill clean. Each time you grill, the cooking rack should be scraped clean with a wire brush. This prevents food from sticking to the cooking rack and reduces the possibility of unpleasant flavors being added to the food.

Barbecue tongs
Tongs allow you to grasp foods without piercing them and allowing their natural juices to escape. They should be long enough so that your hand is at a safe distance from the area immediately above the hot grilling surface.

Grill wok
The grill wok is a four-sided metal basket with multiple symmetrical small holes all over the sides and bottom. It is placed directly on the cooking grate. A grill wok is invaluable for grill stir-frying because its high sides hold the food in place while stirring. Food cannot fall through the small holes, but smoke and grilling aromas pass through them easily.

Meat thermometer

The meat thermometer is an invaluable tool for determining the doneness (rare, medium, well-done) of steaks, roasts, pork, and poultry.

Grilling grid

The grid is a flat, porcelain grate with multiple holes symmetrically placed all over the bottom. Like the grill wok, it is placed directly on the cooking grate. It is excellent for cooking vegetables, or other foods that are too small or fragile to place over a conventional grate with widely spaced bars.

Drip pan

When a recipe calls for the indirect grilling method, a drip pan is placed at the center of the fuel grate, surrounded by charcoal briquettes. This arrangement allows the drippings from the foods to fall into the pan rather than on the coals which might cause flare-ups. You can make your own drip pan by folding two sheets of heavy duty aluminum foil into the shape of a pan.

Hinged wire basket

This accessory consists of two flat wire rectangular grids, hinged on one side. Food is placed between the wire grids and the two sides are closed, keeping the food in place. Adjustable hinged baskets are ideal for grilling hamburgers, fish, steaks, or other kinds of food that may be too fragile to turn.

Metal skewers

Metal skewers are perfect for making kebabs. They are very long and will hold a complete individual serving of meat or fish and vegetables. Unlike wooden skewers, these will not catch fire. Make sure to use an insulated barbecue mitt when touching them. If you use wooden skewers, soak them in water first for at least

30 minutes or overnight to reduce the chance of their catching fire.

Basting brushes

Basting brushes are ideal for brushing marinades or sauces onto food. Make sure to buy one with a long handle and of good quality—there is nothing worse than finding brush hairs on the food!

TECHNIQUES

When cooking with a grill, there are only two basic methods available: food is cooked directly or indirectly over the coals.

Direct method

The direct method is most frequently used when the food to be grilled can be cooked in 30 minutes or less. Using this technique, the food is placed on the cooking rack over the coals and is exposed directly to their heat.

Indirect method

The indirect method is used when the food to be grilled takes longer than 30 minutes to cook and when it is necessary to prevent the food from getting too close to the heat source. A drip pan is placed in the center of the fuel grate and an equal number of briquettes is placed on both sides. After the coals are ashen gray, the cooking grate is positioned over them and the food is placed directly over the drip pan rather than over the coals. If the cooking time is longer than 45 to 60 minutes, it may be necessary to add additional coals.

- Bring meat or fish to room temperature before grilling.
- To seal in the juices when grilling beef, sear it first by cooking it for one minute on each side. Test for doneness by inserting a meat thermometer to measure the temperature of the thickest part of the meat or by observing the color of the beef through a slit made near its center. If the thermometer registers 145 degrees, or if the center is deep pink and the outer portion is brown, then it is *medium rare*. A temperature of 160 degrees or a light pink center and brown outer portion, indicates that it is *medium*. A reading of 170 degrees or beef which appears uniformly brown throughout suggests that the meat is *well done*. For steaks, the best way to determine how long to cook the meat is to follow guidelines that relate to thickness. The Weber's Owner's Guide provides a useful chart for this purpose:

How Long to Cook Steak
(Cooking time in minutes)

	Rare		Medium		Well-Done	
	1st side	2nd side	1st side	2nd side	1st side	2nd side
1 inch thick	2	3	4	4	5	6
1½ inches thick	5	6	7	8	9	10
2 inches thick	7	8	9	9	10	11

- When cooking pork chops, sear the pork for 1 minute on each side. If the chop is ¾-inch thick, cook it for 4 to 5 minutes on each side; if 1½-inches thick, 8 to 10 minutes on each side. Although most recipes suggest cooking pork until a meat thermometer registers 160 degrees, I prefer to cook it until it registers 150 to 155 degrees, because at this temperature the meat is safely cooked but remains more tender and juicy.

• When a recipe calls for a butterflied leg of lamb, ask the butcher to remove the bone in the leg and spread the meat so it lays flat while grilling. The meat is done when a meat thermometer registers 150 degrees for medium-rare and 160 degrees for medium doneness.

• When grilling seafood, a good rule of thumb is that a ¾-inch piece of fish usually requires 8 minutes total cooking time and a 1-inch piece of fish requires 10 minutes or less. To check for doneness, insert a fork into the thickest part of the fish and determine if the flesh has become opaque and somewhat flaky. Remember that when fish is marinated in a sauce that contains lemon juice, the marinating time should be no more than 30 minutes. Otherwise, the lemon juice will initiate chemical changes in the fish similar to cooking.

• All of the chicken recipes in this book call for chicken breasts that are skinned, boned, and have all visible fat removed. When cooking chicken breasts on the grill, I like to turn them frequently to prevent burning and reduce drying. To determine doneness, prick the meat to see if it is white throughout and the juices run clear.

• Grilling time will be affected by the weather. Allow for more time in cold weather.

• When making kebabs, leave a small amount of space between portions of meat on the skewers to assure that each piece is cooked uniformly.

• It is best to coat the grill with a nonstick vegetable spray to prevent food from sticking to the grate. This should be done before the grate is placed over the heat.

• All vegetables should be coated with a cooking oil, preferably olive oil, before grilling as an additional measure to prevent them from sticking to the grill.

CHICKEN

4 SERVINGS

Balsamic vinegar gives the chicken a piquant flavor.
Serve with Grilled Acorn Squash stuffed with Fruited Brown Rice and Quinoa.

Marinade

¼ cup tamari
2 tablespoons balsamic vinegar
½ tablespoon extra-virgin olive oil
2 tablespoons minced fresh basil
½ teaspoon oregano
⅛ teaspoon freshly ground pepper
1 clove garlic, minced

2 chicken breasts (12 ounces each), skinned,
   boned, and halved

To make marinade

Combine tamari, balsamic vinegar, olive oil, basil,
oregano, pepper, and garlic in nonmetal dish. Add
chicken breasts and turn to coat both sides. Cover dish
and refrigerate several hours or overnight, turning
chicken at least once.

WHEN READY TO GRILL

Over hot coals, place chicken breasts on a grill coated with
nonstick vegetable spray. Cover grill and cook 6 to 8 minutes, turning chicken every 3 minutes.

---

161 Calories
27.9 g Protein
1.6 g Carbohydrates
3.9 g Fat
22.0% Calories from Fat
0.0 g Fiber
567 mg Sodium
74 mg Cholesterol

4 SERVINGS

This is a fabulous way to enjoy New Orleans–style Cajun cooking without the usual worry about calories and fat. The spices add a marvelous zest to the chicken that is delicately balanced by the Lemon Dill Yogurt Sauce.
Serve with mugs of chicken gumbo and a fresh fruit salad.

Cajun Spices

2 teaspoons paprika
¼ teaspoon *each* cayenne and salt
⅛ teaspoon *each* freshly ground white pepper
    and black pepper, onion salt, garlic salt, thyme,
    and oregano

Lemon Dill Yogurt Sauce

1 cup plain nonfat yogurt
2 tablespoons fresh lemon juice
2 tablespoons finely chopped fresh dill
½ tablespoon extra-virgin olive oil
½ teaspoon sugar
2 cloves garlic, minced

Blackened Chicken

1 tablespoon fresh lemon juice
1 teaspoon extra-virgin olive oil
1 chicken breast (8 ounces), skinned and boned

4 pita pockets
2 tomatoes, thinly sliced
Shredded lettuce

239 Calories
17.4 g Protein
31.3 g Carbohydrates
5.0 g Fat
18.8% Calories from Fat
1.9 g Fiber
586 mg Sodium
26 mg Cholesterol

To make Cajun spices

Combine paprika, cayenne, salt, white pepper, black pepper, onion salt, garlic salt, thyme, and oregano in a small container and blend well. Set aside.

To make yogurt sauce

Combine yogurt, lemon juice, dill, olive oil, sugar, and garlic in a small bowl and blend well. Refrigerate, covered, for 1 to 2 hours.

To make chicken

Combine lemon juice and olive oil in a nonmetal dish. Add chicken and turn to coat both sides. Cover dish and refrigerate 20 minutes.

WHEN READY TO GRILL

Spread Cajun spices on a plate and coat both sides chicken breast in them. Over hot coals, place chicken breast on grill coated with non-stick vegetable spray. Cover grill and cook 6 to 8 minutes, turning chicken every 3 minutes. Allow chicken to come to room temperature before carving into thin slices.

WHEN READY TO SERVE

Warm pita according to package directions. Cut $1\frac{1}{2}$ inches off one side of pita to make a pocket and fill with sliced chicken, tomatoes, and lettuce. Spoon a generous amount of Lemon Dill Yogurt Sauce over each sandwich.

4 SERVINGS

Grilled chicken was never so easy to make!
Serve with steamed string beans and Grilled Peaches.

Marinade
6 tablespoons Mango Vinaigrette*
3 tablespoons Honeycup prepared mustard

2 chicken breasts (12 ounces each), skinned,
   boned, and halved

To make marinade
Combine Mango Vinaigrette and mustard in a nonmetal dish. Add chicken breasts and turn to coat both sides. Cover dish and refrigerate several hours or overnight, turning chicken breasts at least once.

WHEN READY TO GRILL
Over hot coals, place chicken breasts (reserve marinade) on a grill coated with nonstick vegetable spray. Cover grill and cook 6 to 8 minutes, turning chicken every 3 minutes and brushing with marinade the last 3 minutes.

*Mango Vinaigrette is available at Williams-Sonoma, a food specialty store located throughout the United States or through their mail order catalog.

169 Calories
26.9 g Protein
5.8 g Carbohydrates
3.7 g Fat
19.5% Calories from Fat
0.0 g Fiber
64 mg Sodium
74 mg Cholesterol

4 SERVINGS

The fusion of the mustards and tarragon produces a marvelous blend. It is used first to marinate the chicken breasts and later becomes the crowning touch when it is ladled over the grilled chicken. Serve with wheat pilaf and a fresh fruit salad.

Marinade

3 tablespoons *each* grainy mustard and Dijon mustard

3 tablespoons tarragon vinegar

1½ tablespoons extra-virgin olive oil

1½ tablespoons pineapple juice

¼ teaspoon freshly ground white pepper

2 chicken breasts (12 ounces each), skinned, boned, and halved

To make marinade

Combine mustards, tarragon vinegar, olive oil, pineapple juice, and white pepper in a nonmetal dish. Add chicken breasts and turn to coat both sides. Cover dish and refrigerate several hours or overnight, turning chicken at least once.

WHEN READY TO GRILL

Over hot coals, place chicken (reserve marinade) on a grill coated with nonstick vegetable spray. Cover grill and cook 6 to 8 minutes, turning chicken every 3 minutes.

While chicken is cooking, place reserved marinade in a small, heavy saucepan over moderately low heat and cook until it is heated through. Keep warm.

WHEN READY TO SERVE

Place chicken breasts on individual dinner plates. Spoon 1 to 2 tablespoonfuls of heated sauce over chicken and garnish each serving with a sprig of fresh parsley.

260 Calories
29.0 g Protein
6.1 g Carbohydrates
13.1 g Fat
45.4% Calories from Fat
0.0 g Fiber
577 mg Sodium
74 mg Cholesterol

CHICKEN BREASTS WITH RED PEPPER, SPINACH, AND GOAT CHEESE FILLING

4 SERVINGS

This recipe sounds complicated, but it is really quite easy to make. The red peppers can be grilled ahead of time while the chicken is marinating. The whole chicken roll can be assembled quickly at the last minute.
Serve with Grilled Polenta (page 30), pasta, and a mixed green salad.

2 chicken breasts (12 ounces each), skinned, boned, and halved

Marinade
¼ cup fresh lemon juice
2 tablespoons extra-virgin olive oil
¼ cup minced fresh basil
2 cloves garlic, minced
¼ teaspoon crushed red pepper

2 red peppers
4 spinach leaves
2 ounces goat cheese, cut into 4 pieces

Using a meat mallet, pound the chicken breasts until they are slightly less than ¼ inch thick. Set aside.

To make marinade
Combine lemon juice, olive oil, basil, garlic, and crushed red pepper in a nonmetal dish. Add chicken breasts and turn to coat both sides. Refrigerate, covered, several hours or overnight, turning chicken at least once.

225 Calories
30.1 g Protein
3.6 g Carbohydrates
9.6 g Fat
38.2% Calories from Fat
0.7 g Fiber
119 mg Sodium
80 mg Cholesterol

WHEN READY TO GRILL

Over hot coals, place the red peppers on a grill. Cover grill and cook 14 to 20 minutes or until skins are charred all over, turning peppers as skins blacken. Place the peppers in a plastic bag for 15 minutes.

When the peppers are cool enough to handle, peel away the skin, remove the top and seeds (do not rinse the peppers), and cut each one in half. If not using the peppers immediately, place them in a covered container until ready to use.

Remove chicken breasts from marinade and top each one with a spinach leaf, red pepper half, and ½ ounce goat cheese. Roll up the chicken breast (they do not have to be completely enclosed like an envelope) and secure with a toothpick. Over hot coals, place the chicken breasts on a grill that has been coated with nonstick vegetable spray. Cover the grill and cook 8 to 10 minutes, turning the chicken breasts every 3 minutes. Remove the toothpicks before serving.

4 SERVINGS

The piquant combination of peppercorns and mustard makes an unbelievable marinade. It is wonderful with chicken, and can be used with turkey or beef as well. I like to serve this entree with corn and Roasted Potatoes.

Marinade

¼ cup Grey Poupon peppercorn mustard

2 tablespoons tamari*

1 tablespoon extra-virgin olive oil

1 tablespoon honey

3 cloves garlic, minced

1 piece fresh ginger root, peeled and cut ⅛ inch thick

2 chicken breasts (12 ounces each), skinned, boned, and halved

Roasted Potatoes

2 tablespoons extra-virgin olive oil

1 tablespoon Dijon mustard

1 teaspoon rosemary

½ teaspoon thyme

¼ teaspoon *each* paprika and freshly ground pepper

⅛ teaspoon salt

1½ pounds potatoes, peeled and cut into 1½-inch chunks

362 Calories
31.2 g Protein
29.1 g Carbohydrates
13.3 g Fat
33% Calories from Fat
2.4 g Fiber
691 mg Sodium
74 mg Cholesterol

*Tamari is an intensely flavored soy sauce and is wheat-free. It is available in most Asian food stores.

To make marinade

Combine peppercorn mustard, tamari, olive oil, honey, garlic, and ginger root in a nonmetal dish. Add chicken breasts and turn to coat both sides. Cover dish and refrigerate several hours or overnight, turning chicken breasts at least once.

Preheat oven to 400 degrees.

To make roasted potatoes

Combine 2 tablespoons olive oil, Dijon mustard, rosemary, thyme, paprika, pepper, and salt and blend well. Add potatoes and toss to coat all over. Place the potato mixture in a 10 × 15-inch jelly roll pan that has been heavily coated with nonstick vegetable spray. Bake for 45 minutes or until fork tender, turning potatoes every 15 minutes.

Over hot coals, place chicken breasts on a grill coated with non-stick vegetable spray. Cover grill and cook 6 to 8 minutes, turning chicken every 3 minutes.

4 SERVINGS

Raspberry-flavored grilled chicken and Raspberry Vinaigrette combine to make a colorful and refreshing salad to enjoy on a hot summer day.

Marinade
½ cup raspberry vinegar
2 tablespoons Dijon mustard
¼ teaspoon freshly ground white pepper

2 chicken breasts (10 ounces each), skinned, boned, and halved

Raspberry Vinaigrette
1 shallot (1 ounce), chopped
3 tablespoons raspberry vinegar
1 tablespoon Dijon mustard
⅛ teaspoon *each* salt and freshly ground white pepper
¼ cup extra-virgin olive oil

4 cups combined red leaf and romaine lettuce
2 pears, seeded and cut into wedges
Raspberries

318 Calories
24.0 g Protein
18.0 g Carbohydrates
17.6 g Fat
50% Calories from Fat
3.1 g Fiber
325 mg Sodium
61 mg Cholesterol

To make marinade

Combine raspberry vinegar, mustard, and white pepper in a nonmetal dish. Add chicken breasts and turn to coat both sides. Cover dish and refrigerate several hours or overnight, turning chicken at least once.

To make Raspberry Vinaigrette

In work bowl of food processor fitted with a metal blade, process shallot until finely chopped. Add raspberry vinegar, mustard, salt, and pepper and process until blended. Add olive oil in a slow steady stream and process until well blended. Set aside.

WHEN READY TO GRILL

Over hot coals, place chicken breasts on a grill coated with nonstick vegetable spray. Cover grill and cook 6 to 8 minutes, turning chicken every 3 minutes. Allow chicken to come to room temperature. When cool, carve the chicken into ¼-inch-thick slices.

WHEN READY TO SERVE

Divide lettuce among four salad plates. Place chicken on lettuce so it resembles an open fan, leaving spaces in between for slices of pears. Spoon 1½ to 2 tablespoons raspberry vinaigrette over each salad and garnish with fresh raspberries, if available.

6 SERVINGS

Pizza cooked on a grill is a new taste sensation you will definitely enjoy!
It is at its best when flavored with an Asian sauce and topped with grilled
chicken and slivered red, orange, and yellow peppers.

Sauce
½ cup hoisin sauce
1 teaspoon *each* teriyaki sauce, soy sauce, and
    Szechwan chili sauce*
½ teaspoon oyster sauce
1 teaspoon *each* minced garlic and fresh
    ginger root

1 chicken breast (12 ounces), skinned and boned

3 tandoori style naan* (Indian bread)
¾ cup shredded mozzarella cheese
6 tablespoons *each* slivered red, yellow, and
    orange pepper
¾ cup sliced fresh shiitake mushrooms
¾ cup shredded mozzarella cheese

*Szechwan chili sauce and Tandoori style naan are available
in most Asian or health food stores.

327 Calories
23.8 g Protein
34.9 g Carbohydrates
10.4 g Fat
29% Calories from Fat
2.3 g Fiber
851 mg Sodium
41 mg Cholesterol

Prepare the grill by placing the charcoal on one half of the charcoal grate. This will enable you to move the pizza away from the heat source while it is cooking.

To make sauce
Combine hoisin sauce, teriyaki sauce, soy sauce, Szechwan chili sauce, oyster sauce, garlic, and ginger root in a small bowl.

WHEN READY TO GRILL
Brush both sides of the chicken breast with some of the sauce. Over hot coals, place chicken breast on a grill coated with nonstick vegetable spray. Cover grill and cook 6 to 8 minutes, turning chicken every 3 minutes. Allow chicken to cool for 5 minutes before cutting it into slivers.

To prepare pizzas
Brush remaining sauce on each piece of naan. Distribute 4 tablespoons mozzarella cheese over *each* naan and top with peppers, mushrooms, grilled chicken slivers, and 4 tablespoons mozzarella cheese.

Place 1 to 2 pizzas (depending on the size of grill) over coals. Cover grill and cook 1 minute. Move pizza with tongs over to the side of grill where there are no coals. Continue to cook 10 minutes or until the cheese has melted. Remove pizza with a very wide spatula.

6 SERVINGS

The fusion of the smoky flavor of the chicken and the hot spices creates an exceptional chili. Depending on dietary restrictions, the chili is delicious topped either with fatfree or light shredded cheddar cheese and sour cream, in addition to chopped green onions and salsa.

½ pound small white beans
½ pound white northern beans
3 cans (14½ ounces each) fatfree chicken broth
1 large onion, chopped
4 cloves garlic, minced
1 yellow pepper, chopped
2 tablespoons chopped cilantro
1 tablespoon *each* cumin, oregano, and freshly
 ground white pepper
½ teaspoon coriander
¼ teaspoon salt
⅛ teaspoon cayenne

2 chicken breasts (12 ounces each), skinned
 and boned

1 can (4½ ounces), minced green chiles
2 tablespoons chopped banana pepper*

*Banana peppers are large, yellow peppers with a mild flavor.

381 Calories
43.2 g Protein
43.2 g Carbohydrates
4.1 g Fat
10% Calories from Fat
7.4 g Fiber
1247 mg Sodium
74 mg Cholesterol

Place beans in a large mixing bowl and add enough water to completely cover beans. Set aside for 24 hours.

Drain beans and rinse well. Place beans in a Dutch oven and add 2 cans chicken broth, onion, garlic, yellow pepper, cilantro, cumin, oregano, white pepper, coriander, salt, and cayenne. Bring to a boil over moderate heat. Lower heat, cover, and simmer 4 hours, adding more chicken broth, if necessary. While chili is cooking, grill the chicken breasts.

When the chili has cooked for 4 hours, add the grilled chicken cubes, remaining chicken broth, green chiles, and banana pepper and blend well. Taste for seasoning. Cover and cook an additional 1 hour. The chili can be served immediately or allowed to sit in the refrigerator for 24 hours to let the flavors blend.

WHEN READY TO GRILL

Over hot coals, place chicken breasts on a grill coated with nonstick vegetable spray. Cover grill and cook 6 to 8 minutes, turning chicken every 3 minutes. Allow the chicken to cool for 10 minutes. Cut the chicken into 1-inch cubes and set aside.

6 SERVINGS

This is a very light and refreshing salad that is perfect summer fare. Start the meal off with a mug of chilled soup and serve the salad with Pineapple Muffins (a recipe from my cookbook 101 Great Lowfat Desserts*).*

Dressing

2 tablespoons cider vinegar

3 tablespoons sugar

$\frac{1}{4}$ teaspoon *each* salt, Accent, and freshly ground pepper

$\frac{1}{4}$ cup canola oil

3 tablespoons sesame seeds

2 chicken breasts (8 ounces each), skinned and boned

4 teaspoons Szechwan chili sauce

1 head iceberg lettuce

2 cups bean sprouts

4 carrots, cut into long strips

4 green onions, thinly sliced

1 can (8 ounces) sliced water chestnuts, drained

1 can (8 ounces) bamboo shoots, drained

Pineapple Muffins

1 can (20 ounces) crushed pine-apple

3 cups flour

1 cup sugar

1 tablespoon baking powder

$\frac{1}{4}$ teaspoon salt

1 cup skim milk

3 egg whites

1 teaspoon vanilla

264 Calories
16.1 g Protein
21.1 g Carbohydrates
13.5 g Fat
45.9% Calories from Fat
3.4 g Fiber
215 mg Sodium
33 mg Cholesterol

To make dressing

In work bowl of food processor fitted with metal blade, combine cider vinegar, sugar, salt, Accent, and pepper and process until blended. Add canola oil in a slow steady stream and process until well blended. Set aside.

Preheat oven to 350 degrees. Place sesame seeds in a small pan and bake for 10 to 15 minutes or until golden brown. Set aside.

WHEN READY TO GRILL

Brush each side of chicken breast with ½ teaspoon Szechwan sauce. Over hot coals, place chicken on a grill coated with nonstick vegetable spray. Cover grill and cook 6 to 8 minutes, turning chicken every 3 minutes. Allow chicken to cool. Cut chicken into cubes and set aside.

In a large salad bowl, tear lettuce into bite-size pieces. Add grilled chicken cubes, sesame seeds, bean sprouts, carrots, green onions, water chestnuts, and bamboo shoots and toss to blend. Add dressing and toss until well blended. Serve immediately.

To make muffins

Place pineapple in a strainer over a bowl. Reserve ⅔ cup pineapple juice and the pineapple.

Combine flour, sugar, baking powder, and salt in a large mixing bowl. In a separate medium bowl, combine pineapple, reserved pineapple juice, skim milk, egg whites, and vanilla and blend well. Add pineapple mixture to dry ingredients and mix with a fork until just blended.

Spoon batter just to the tops of muffin cups that have been coated with nonstick vegetable spray. Bake 20 minutes, or until golden. Immediately remove muffins from pan. When muffins are cool, store in an airtight container. These muffins taste best when allowed to sit for 24 hours. Makes 20 muffins.

4 SERVINGS

*This is a quick and easy way to prepare chicken
and the result is a very moist and flavorful entree.
Serve with your favorite pasta dish and a tossed salad.*

2 chicken breasts (12 ounces each), skinned,
   boned, and halved
$\frac{1}{4}$ cup *each* Dijon mustard and fresh lemon juice
2 teaspoons Worcestershire sauce

Place chicken breasts in a nonmetal dish and spread the top of each one with $\frac{1}{2}$ tablespoon mustard. Turn chicken over and spread each one with $\frac{1}{2}$ tablespoon mustard. Pour 1 tablespoon lemon juice and $\frac{1}{2}$ teaspoon Worcestershire sauce over each chicken breast. Cover dish and refrigerate several hours or overnight.

WHEN READY TO GRILL
Over hot coals, place chicken breasts on a grill coated with nonstick vegetable spray. Cover grill and cook 6 to 8 minutes, turning chicken every 3 minutes.

174 Calories
28.0 g Protein
2.7 g Carbohydrates
5.1 g Fat
26% Calories from Fat
0.0 g Fiber
489 mg Sodium
74 mg Cholesterol

4 SERVINGS

The marinade is a wonderful blend of lemon juice and herbs. It can also be used with pork or poultry. Serve with Grilled Crookneck Squash and lemon rice pilaf.

Marinade

¼ cup fresh lemon juice

3 tablespoons finely chopped parsley

1 tablespoon extra-virgin olive oil

1 teaspoon finely grated lemon peel

1 teaspoon thyme

¾ teaspoon savory

½ teaspoon rosemary

¼ teaspoon marjoram

2 whole chicken breasts (12 ounces each),
    skinned, boned, and halved

To make marinade

Combine lemon juice, parsley, olive oil, lemon peel, thyme, savory, rosemary, and marjoram in a nonmetal dish and blend well. Add chicken breasts and turn to coat both sides. Cover dish and refrigerate several hours or overnight, turning chicken at least once.

WHEN READY TO GRILL

Over hot coals, place chicken breasts on a grill coated with non-stick vegetable spray. Cover grill and cook 6 to 8 minutes, turning every 3 minutes.

163 Calories

27.1 g Protein

1.0 g Carbohydrates

4.9 g Fat

27% Calories from Fat

0.1 g Fiber

65 mg Sodium

74 mg Cholesterol

4 SERVINGS

The exotic taste of this flavorful dish belies its simplicity!
Serve with Roasted Pepper Salad (page 278) and Japanese Eggplant.

Marinade
½ cup fresh lemon juice
1 tablespoon extra-virgin olive oil
8 cloves garlic, minced
1¼ teaspoons freshly ground pepper

2 chicken breasts (12 ounces each), skinned,
    boned, and halved

To make marinade
Combine lemon juice, olive oil, garlic, and pepper in a nonmetal dish. Add chicken breasts and turn to coat both sides. Cover dish and refrigerate several hours or overnight, turning chicken at least once.

WHEN READY TO GRILL
Over hot coals, place chicken (reserve marinade) on a grill coated with nonstick vegetable spray. Cover and cook 6 to 8 minutes, turning chicken every 3 minutes and brushing with reserved marinade.

167 Calories
27.2 g Protein
2.4 g Carbohydrates
4.9 g Fat
26% Calories from Fat
0.1 g Fiber
65 mg Sodium
74 mg Cholesterol

4 SERVINGS

This is a nicely spiced chicken entree that is moist and highly flavorful. Serve with Raita (page 124), basmati rice, and your favorite kind of Indian bread such as naan or papadum (both are available at Asian food stores).

Marinade

½ cup pineapple juice
1 tablespoon extra-virgin olive oil
2 teaspoons curry powder
1 teaspoon *each* turmeric, coriander, and freshly
    ground pepper
¼ teaspoon *each* salt, nutmeg, and cinnamon

2 chicken breasts (12 ounces each), skinned,
    boned, and halved

To make marinade

Combine pineapple juice, olive oil, curry, turmeric, coriander, pepper, salt, nutmeg, and cinnamon in a non-metal dish. Add chicken breasts and turn to coat both sides. Cover dish and refrigerate several hours or overnight, turning chicken at least once.

WHEN READY TO GRILL

Over hot coals, place chicken on a grill coated with non-stick vegetable spray. Cover grill and cook 6 to 8 minutes, turning chicken every 3 minutes.

172 Calories
27.1 g Protein
2.9 g Carbohydrates
5.0 g Fat
26% Calories from Fat
0.2 g Fiber
131 mg Sodium
74 mg Cholesterol

4 SERVINGS

This spicy chicken has a wonderful southwestern flavor. Serve it with Corn Relish on the side, Mexican Rice (page 50), and a jicama and kiwi salad with a citrus vinaigrette.

Marinade

1 cup plain nonfat yogurt

¼ cup fresh lime juice

¼ teaspoon *each* cumin, chili powder, cayenne, and paprika

⅛ teaspoon *each* coriander and freshly ground pepper

2 tablespoons minced cilantro

1 clove garlic, minced

1 serrano pepper*, seeded and minced

2 chicken breasts (12 ounces each), skinned, boned, and halved

Corn Relish

2 cups fresh or frozen corn kernels

2 cans (14½ ounces each) fatfree chicken broth

¼ cup diced red pepper

2 serrano peppers, seeded and diced*

½ teaspoon marjoram

¼ teaspoon *each* cumin and freshly ground pepper

2 tablespoons light margarine

2 tablespoons packed, chopped cilantro

*The seeds of the serrano pepper are very hot. To avoid burning your skin, wear rubber or latex gloves when removing the seeds. Immediately wash the knife, cutting surface, and gloves when finished.

To make marinade

Combine yogurt, lime juice, cumin, chili powder, cayenne, paprika, coriander, pepper, cilantro, garlic, and serrano pepper in a nonmetal dish. Add chicken and turn to coat both sides. Cover dish and refrigerate several hours or overnight, turning at least once.

To make Corn Relish

Combine corn, chicken broth, red pepper, serrano peppers, marjoram, cumin, and pepper in a medium saucepan over moderate heat. Cook 20 to 25 minutes or until most of the liquid has evaporated. Add margarine and stir until blended. Add cilantro and blend well. Keep warm.

WHEN READY TO GRILL
Over hot coals, place chicken on grill coated with nonstick vegetable spray. Cover grill, cooking 6 to 8 minutes, turning chicken every 3 minutes.

166 Calories
28.9 g Protein
3.9 g Carbohydrates
3.2 g Fat
17% Calories from Fat
0.2 g Fiber
89 mg Sodium
74 mg Cholesterol

4 SERVINGS

I like to serve this extra spicy chicken with gazpacho,
Grilled Corn in the Husk, and a mixed vegetable salad.

Marinade

2 tablespoons fresh lemon juice

1 tablespoon extra-virgin olive oil

4 cloves garlic, minced

½ teaspoon *each* rosemary and freshly
  ground pepper

¼ teaspoon basil

⅛ teaspoon crushed red pepper

2 chicken breasts (12 ounces each), skinned,
  boned, and halved

Gazpacho

1 medium yellow onion, peeled and quartered

1 large red pepper, seeded and cut into
  large pieces

1 small cucumber, peeled and cut into 2-inch
  lengths

1 teaspoon Worcestershire sauce

½ teaspoon hot pepper sauce

1 teaspoon freshly ground pepper

4 cups tomato juice

1 small cucumber, cubed

1 large tomato, cubed

1 small yellow pepper, cubed

1 small red pepper, cubed

4 green onions, thinly sliced

271 Calories
31.3 g Protein
26.3 g Carbohydrates
5.5 g Fat
18% Calories from Fat
4.7 g Fiber
995 mg Sodium
74 mg Cholesterol

To make marinade

Combine lemon juice, olive oil, garlic, rosemary, pepper, basil, and crushed red pepper in a nonmetal dish. Place chicken breasts in dish and turn to coat both sides. Cover dish and refrigerate several hours or overnight, turning chicken at least once.

To make gazpacho

In a food processor fitted with a metal blade, process onion, red pepper, and cucumber until finely chopped. Add Worcestershire sauce, hot pepper sauce, ground pepper, and tomato juice and process until smooth. Remove mixture to a 1-quart pitcher and refrigerate, covered, for several hours or overnight.

WHEN READY TO GRILL

Over hot coals, place chicken on grill coated with nonstick vegetable spray. Cover and cook 6 to 8 minutes, turning chicken every 3 minutes.

WHEN READY TO SERVE

Fill individual serving dishes with cubed cucumbers, tomatoes, yellow and red peppers, and green onions and arrange dishes around pitcher of soup. Encourage your guests to make their own gazpacho by filling their bowls or mugs with desired vegetables and soup. Additional tomato juice can be added to the pitcher if soup is too thick.

4 SERVINGS

*This is a family favorite because its wonderful array of ingredients
makes the chicken so flavorful. Serve with fresh pasta and
a combination of sautéed snow peas and red pepper slivers.*

Marinade

¼ cup soy sauce

2 tablespoons extra-virgin olive oil

1 tablespoon hoisin sauce

2 teaspoons dry mustard

1 teaspoon freshly ground lemon pepper

4 cloves garlic, minced

4 green onions, minced

2 tablespoons sesame seeds

2 whole chicken breasts (12 ounces each),
   skinned, boned, and halved

To make marinade

Combine soy sauce, olive oil, hoisin sauce, mustard,
lemon pepper, garlic, green onions, and sesame seeds in
a nonmetal dish. Place chicken breasts in dish and turn
to coat both sides. Cover dish and refrigerate several
hours or overnight, turning chicken at least once.

WHEN READY TO GRILL

Over hot coals, place chicken on a grill coated with nonstick vegetable spray. Cover grill and cook 6 to 8 minutes,
turning chicken every 3 minutes.

201 Calories
28.4 g Protein
3.0 g Carbohydrates
7.9 g Fat
35% Calories from Fat
0.4 g Fiber
742 mg Sodium
74 mg Cholesterol

4 SERVINGS

The spicy yogurt marinade makes the chicken breasts moist and flavorful.
Serve with Cranberry Chutney (page 40), steamed basmati rice, and a fresh fruit salad.

Marinade
1 cup plain nonfat yogurt
2 tablespoons minced shallots
1½ teaspoons coriander
½ teaspoon *each* cinnamon, cardamom, turmeric,
    ginger, and freshly ground pepper
¼ teaspoon *each* crushed red pepper and salt

2 chicken breasts (12 ounces each), skinned,
    boned, and halved

To make marinade
Combine yogurt, shallots, coriander, cinnamon, cardamom, turmeric, ginger, pepper, crushed red pepper,
and salt in a nonmetal dish. Add chicken and turn to
coat both sides. Cover dish and refrigerate several
hours or overnight.

WHEN READY TO GRILL
Over hot coals, place chicken breasts on a grill coated with
nonstick vegetable spray. Cover grill and cook 6 to 8 minutes, turning chicken every 3 minutes.

164 Calories
28.8 g Protein
3.1 g Carbohydrates
3.3 g Fat
18% Calories from Fat
0.2 g Fiber
153 mg Sodium
74 mg Cholesterol

4 SERVINGS

While cooking the chicken on the grill, offer your guests mugs of Gazpacho (page 26). Serve the spicy chicken with Mexican Rice (page 50), an orange and jicama salad with lime vinaigrette, and Grilled Polenta.

Marinade

1 cup plain nonfat yogurt
2 tablespoons fresh lime juice
1 clove garlic, minced
1 teaspoon *each* oregano and cumin
$\frac{1}{4}$ teaspoon *each* salt and freshly ground pepper
$\frac{1}{8}$ teaspoon *each* paprika and chili powder

2 chicken breasts (12 ounces each), skinned, boned, and halved

Grilled Polenta

1 cup cold water
1 cup cornmeal
$\frac{1}{4}$ teaspoon salt
$2\frac{1}{4}$ cups boiling water
2 tablespoons light margarine

164 Calories
28.8 g Protein
3.1 g Carbohydrates
3.3 g Fat
17.9% Calories from Fat
0.1 g Fiber
154 mg Sodium
74 mg Cholesterol

To make marinade

Combine yogurt, lime juice, garlic, oregano, cumin, salt, pepper, paprika, and chili powder in a nonmetal dish. Add chicken and turn to coat both sides. Cover dish and refrigerate several hours or overnight.

To make Grilled Polenta

Combine 1 cup cold water, cornmeal, and salt in a heavy medium-size saucepan. *Slowly* add 2¼ cups *boiling* water, stirring frequently. Place saucepan over low heat and cook 25 minutes or until very thick, stirring frequently. Add margarine and blend well. Spread polenta into a 9-inch square baking pan coated with nonstick vegetable spray and let it come to room temperature. Cover pan and refrigerate several hours or overnight.

WHEN READY TO GRILL

Cut polenta into six serving-size pieces and place on a grilling grid* heavily coated with nonstick vegetable spray. Place grid on grill over hot coals and cook, covered, for 10 minutes on each side or until golden brown.

Place chicken on a grill coated with nonstick vegetable spray. Cover grill and cook 6 to 8 minutes, turning every 3 minutes.

*A grilling grid is described in the *Helpful Guidelines* section.

4 SERVINGS

An elegant dish to serve at a formal dinner. A medley of flavors and texture that is richly enhanced by the essence of tarragon. Serve the chicken on a bed of wild rice and accompany it with a Spinach and Strawberry Salad.

Spinach and Strawberry Salad

¼ cup sugar
¼ cup white wine vinegar
1 teaspoon Dijon mustard
¼ teaspoon salt
5 tablespoons canola oil
1 tablespoon poppy seeds

1½ bunches fresh spinach, washed and stems removed
1½ pints fresh strawberries, hulled and sliced

Marinade

¼ cup fresh lemon juice
1 tablespoon extra-virgin olive oil
¼ teaspoon *each* salt, freshly ground pepper, and paprika
⅛ teaspoon thyme
1 garlic clove, minced

2 chicken breasts (12 ounces each), skinned, boned, and halved

Mushroom Sauce

1 tablespoon light margarine
2 cups sliced mushrooms
3 tablespoons minced shallots
¼ cup chopped green onion
2 tablespoons flour
Fatfree chicken broth
¼ cup dry white wine
¾ cup fatfree chicken broth
½ tablespoon cornstarch
¾ cup fatfree chicken broth
½ tablespoon tarragon
¼ teaspoon thyme
⅛ teaspoon *each* salt and freshly ground pepper
parsley

To make marinade

Combine lemon juice, olive oil, salt, pepper, paprika, thyme, and garlic in a nonmetal dish. Add chicken breasts and turn to coat both sides. Cover dish and refrigerate several hours or overnight, turning chicken at least once.

To make Mushroom Sauce

Coat a medium saucepan with nonstick vegetable spray and place over moderate heat. Add margarine and cook until it begins to sizzle. Add mushrooms, shallots, and green onions and cook 5 minutes or until mushrooms are brown. Remove vegetables to a dish and set aside. Add flour to saucepan and stir in enough broth, 1 tablespoon at a time, to make a paste. Cook 3 minutes. Add wine and ¾ cup chicken broth and cook until mixture boils, stirring occasionally. Combine cornstarch, ¾ cup chicken broth, tarragon, thyme, salt, and pepper in a small bowl and blend until smooth. Add tarragon mixture to saucepan and blend well. Cook until mixture comes to a boil. Add vegetables and blend well. Keep warm while preparing chicken breasts.

To make Spinach and Strawberry Salad

Arrange spinach and strawberries among four salad plates and drizzle the poppy seed dressing over the salad.

To make poppy seed dressing

In work bowl of food processor fitted with a metal blade, process sugar, white wine vinegar, mustard, and ¼ teaspoon salt until blended. In a slow steady stream, add oil and process until well blended. Add poppy seeds and blend well.

WHEN READY TO GRILL

Over hot coals, place chicken breasts on a grill coated with nonstick vegetable spray. Cover grill and cook 6 to 8 minutes, turning every 3 minutes.

WHEN READY TO SERVE

On each dinner plate, place a chicken breast on a bed of wild rice. Spoon ¼ cup mushroom sauce over top and garnish each serving with a sprig of fresh parsley.

225 Calories
29.1 g Protein
9.2 g Carbohydrates
6.6 g Fat
26% Calories from Fat
1.0 g Fiber
453 mg Sodium
74 mg Cholesterol

4 SERVINGS

*This delicious dish is a cornucopia of colors and textures. The marinade
is sensational and would also be great in combination with pork or turkey.
Serve with wheat pilaf and a combination of green beans and mandarin oranges.*

Marinade

½ cup *each* tamari and rice wine

2 tablespoons *each* fresh lemon juice and honey

2 tablespoons toasted sesame seeds

½ tablespoon extra-virgin olive oil

1 teaspoon sesame oil

1 teaspoon dry mustard

½ teaspoon freshly ground pepper

2 dashes hot pepper sauce

2 cloves garlic, minced

1 piece fresh ginger root, peeled and cut
   ¼ inch thick

2 chicken breasts (12 ounces each), skinned,
   boned, and cut into 1½-inch cubes

Kebab Vegetables

8 mushroom caps

1 yellow pepper, cut into eight 1½-inch pieces

4 green onions, each cut into two 2-inch lengths

8 cherry tomatoes

270 Calories
31.3 g Protein
19.7 g Carbohydrates
5.9 g Fat
20% Calories from Fat
2.5 g Fiber
1080 mg Sodium
74 mg Cholesterol

To make marinade

Combine tamari, rice wine, lemon juice, honey, sesame seeds, olive oil, sesame oil, mustard, pepper, hot pepper sauce, garlic, and ginger root in a nonmetal dish. Add chicken cubes and turn to evenly coat. Cover dish and refrigerate several hours or overnight, turning chicken at least once.

WHEN READY TO GRILL

Alternate pieces of chicken, mushrooms, yellow pepper, green onions, and tomatoes on skewers. Over hot coals, place skewers on a grill coated with nonstick vegetable spray. Cover grill and cook 6 to 8 minutes, turning chicken every 3 minutes.

4 SERVINGS

Tandoori chicken is an Indian dish traditionally baked in a special oven (tandoor); however, this recipe has been altered so it can be made on an ordinary grill. The chicken is very spicy and hot. Serve with an Indian vegetable dish, yogurt, and naan, a tender Indian flat bread available in most Asian food stores.

WHEN READY TO GRILL

Over hot coals, place chicken breasts on a grill coated with non-stick vegetable spray. Cover grill and cook 6 to 8 minutes, turning every 3 minutes.

160 Calories
28.0 g Protein
3.0 g Carbohydrates
3.3 g Fat
19% Calories from Fat
0.3 g Fiber
209 mg Sodium
74 mg Cholesterol

Marinade

5 cloves garlic
1 tablespoon minced fresh ginger root
2 tablespoons fresh lemon juice
1 tablespoon garam masala*
1 teaspoon cayenne
½ teaspoon *each* paprika and salt
¼ teaspoon saffron
½ cup plain nonfat yogurt

2 chicken breasts (12 ounces each), skinned, boned, and halved

In work bowl of food processor fitted with a metal blade, process garlic and ginger root until finely chopped. Add lemon juice, garam masala, cayenne, paprika, salt, and saffron and process until smooth. Add yogurt and process just to blend. Transfer yogurt mixture to a nonmetal dish. Place chicken breasts in marinade and turn chicken to coat both sides. Cover dish and refrigerate several hours or overnight.

*Garam masala is available in most Asian food stores. To make your own: combine 1 tablespoon *each* ground cardamom and cinnamon, 1 teaspoon *each* ground cloves, cayenne, and cumin, ¼ teaspoon *each* mace and ground nutmeg in a small container and mix well. Store in a tightly closed container.

TURKEY

4 SERVINGS

The selection of turkey cuts now available makes it easy to enjoy this lowfat meat in a variety of interesting and delicious ways. Serve this quick and easy turkey entree with wheat pilaf and grilled Pineapple Rings.

Marinade

¼ cup soy sauce

2 tablespoons honey

1 clove garlic, minced

1 piece fresh ginger root, peeled and sliced
    ½ inch thick

⅛ teaspoon hot pepper sauce

1 turkey breast (1 pound), cut into ¾-inch cubes

1 green pepper, cut into ¼-inch slices

1 cup thinly sliced mushrooms

1½ cups fresh pineapple chunks

To make marinade

Combine soy sauce, honey, garlic, ginger root, and hot pepper sauce in a nonmetal dish. Add turkey and toss to coat pieces. Cover dish and refrigerate several hours.

While turkey is cooking, add vegetable mixture to reserved marinade and blend well.

Add vegetables, pineapple, and marinade to wok and stir-fry for 1 minute. Cover grill and cook 2 minutes.

WHEN READY TO GRILL

Over hot coals, place a grilling wok that has been coated with non-stick vegetable spray. Add turkey (reserve marinade and discard ginger root) and stir-fry for 1 minute. Cover grill and cook 2 minutes. Repeat stir fry and cooking process one more time.

211 Calories

26.9 g Protein

19.1 g Carbohydrates

3.1 g Fat

13% Calories from Fat

1.2 g Fiber

1085 mg Sodium

58 mg Cholesterol

4 SERVINGS

The zesty marinade makes the turkey exceptionally juicy and flavorful. Serve with Cranberry Chutney, grilled Sweet Potatoes, and a combination of peas and small onions.

Cranberry Chutney

1 cup sugar
1 cup cold water
½ cup chopped onions
4 whole cloves
1 teaspoon cinnamon
½ teaspoon salt
¼ cup distilled white vinegar
2 cups fresh or frozen cranberries
½ cup raisins
½ cup chopped dried dates
¼ cup chopped preserved ginger
¼ cup firmly packed dark brown sugar

Marinade

1 tablespoon Dijon mustard
1½ tablespoons extra-virgin olive oil
1 teaspoon thyme
½ teaspoon *each* salt, pepper, poultry seasoning, savory, and sage
¼ teaspoon paprika

1 fresh turkey breast (3 pounds), split

392 Calories
55.1 g Protein
21.5 g Carbohydrates
8.8 g Fat
20.3% Calories from Fat
2.0 g Fiber
370 mg Sodium
126 mg Cholesterol

*The nutritional analysis is based on using ¼ cup of chutney per serving.

To make Cranberry Chutney

Combine sugar, water, onions, cloves, cinnamon, salt, and vinegar in a medium-size saucepan over moderate heat. Bring to boil and simmer 5 minutes. Add cranberries, raisins, dates, ginger, and brown sugar and blend well. Simmer 10 to 12 minutes. Remove saucepan from heat and bring to room temperature. Refrigerate cranberry chutney in a covered container.

To make marinade

Combine mustard, olive oil, thyme, salt, pepper, poultry seasoning, savory, sage, and paprika in a small bowl. Rub mixture over top of turkey.

WHEN READY TO GRILL

Prepare a grill with a drip pan in the center of the lower grate and place an equal number of briquettes on both sides. When coals are hot, place the turkey centered over the drip pan on a grill coated with a nonstick vegetable spray. Cover grill and cook 2 to 2½ hours, or until turkey is no longer pink inside when a knife is inserted into the thickest part and a meat thermometer registers 170 degrees.

4 SERVINGS

The sweetness of honey in the marinade is complemented by the curry.
It is also an excellent marinade for chicken breasts. Serve with Grilled Sweet Potatoes
and a Spinach and Strawberry Salad (page 32).

Marinade
⅓ cup honey
2 tablespoons tamari
1 tablespoon Dijon mustard
2 teaspoons curry powder
¼ teaspoon powdered ginger

4 turkey tenderloins (6 ounces each)

To make marinade
Combine honey, tamari, mustard, curry, and ginger in a nonmetal dish and blend well. Set aside.

Using a meat mallet, pound the turkey tenderloins until they are slightly less than ½ inch thick. Place tenderloins in marinade and turn to coat both sides. Cover dish and refrigerate several hours or overnight, turning turkey at least once.

WHEN READY TO GRILL
Over hot coals, place turkey on a grill coated with nonstick vegetable spray. Cover grill and cook 6 to 8 minutes, turning turkey every 3 minutes.

243 Calories
37.6 g Protein
11.9 g Carbohydrates
4.3 g Fat
16% Calories from Fat
0.1 g Fiber
383 mg Sodium
85 mg Cholesterol

4 SERVINGS

This easy-to-prepare marinade creates a flavorful and exceptionally moist turkey tenderloin. Serve with Grilled Acorn Squash and steamed broccoli.

Marinade
¼ cup Dijon mustard
2 tablespoons honey
2 tablespoons firmly packed dark brown sugar
1 tablespoon white wine vinegar
½ tablespoon tamari
½ teaspoon sesame oil

1½ pounds turkey tenderloins

To make marinade
Combine mustard, honey, brown sugar, white wine vinegar, tamari, and sesame oil in a nonmetal dish.

Divide turkey tenderloins into four pieces. Using a meat mallet, pound each tenderloin until it is ½ inch thick. Place tenderloins in marinade and turn to coat both sides. Cover dish and refrigerate several hours or overnight, turning turkey at least once.

WHEN READY TO GRILL
Over hot coals, place turkey on a grill coated with nonstick vegetable spray. Cover grill and cook 6 to 8 minutes, turning turkey every 3 minutes.

241 Calories
37.9 g Protein
8.4 g Carbohydrates
5.3 g Fat
20% Calories from Fat
0.0 g Fiber
341 mg Sodium
86 mg Cholesterol

12 SERVINGS

*This is a wonderfully easy way to prepare turkey. I asked
my butcher to remove the bones and skin from a fresh turkey breast,
and all I had to do was create a zesty marinade to complement it.
Serve with Grilled Yams and Ginger-Pineapple Sauce (page 154).*

Marinade

6 tablespoons honey

4½ tablespoons kecap manis*

2 tablespoons extra-virgin olive oil

2 tablespoons Dijon mustard

2¼ teaspoons Worcestershire sauce

¾ teaspoon *each* poultry seasoning and freshly
   ground pepper

¼ teaspoon crushed red pepper

1 turkey breast (6 pounds), boned and skinned

1 can (14½ ounces) chicken broth

***Kecap manis is an Indonesian condiment available in most
Asian food stores.**

274 Calories
36.8 g Protein
18.3 g Carbohydrates
6.6 g Fat
21.5% Calories from Fat
0.0 g Fiber
420 mg Sodium
84 mg Cholesterol

To make marinade

Combine honey, kecap manis, olive oil, mustard, Worcestershire sauce, poultry seasoning, pepper, and crushed red pepper in a large nonmetal dish. Add turkey breast and turn to coat all over. Cover dish and refrigerate several hours or overnight, turning turkey at least once.

WHEN READY TO GRILL

Prepare a grill with a large drip pan in the center of the lower grate and place an equal number of briquettes on both sides of pan. When coals are hot, pour chicken broth into drip pan and place the turkey (reserve marinade) directly over it on a grill coated with nonstick vegetable spray. Cover grill and cook 40 to 50 minutes or until a meat thermometer registers 170 degrees, turning turkey every 8 minutes and brushing with reserved marinade. Allow the turkey to sit for 5 minutes before carving it into thin slices.

4 SERVINGS

*The marinade is a masterful balance of Asian flavorings. It can be used
with pork or chicken, but it goes exceptionally well with turkey.
Serve with mango muffins and a salad of mixed baby greens.*

WHEN READY TO GRILL

Over hot coals, place turkey (reserve marinade) on a grill coated with nonstick vegetable spray. Cover grill and cook 6 to 8 minutes, turning turkey every 3 minutes and brushing with marinade.

242 Calories
37.9 g Protein
6.5 g Carbohydrates
6.3 g Fat
23.3% Calories from Fat
0.1 g Fiber
436 mg Sodium
86 mg Cholesterol

Marinade

½ cup pineapple juice
2 tablespoons soy sauce
2 tablespoons Honeycup prepared mustard
1 tablespoon *each* extra-virgin olive oil, honey, and hoisin sauce
½ tablespoon oyster sauce
½ teaspoon sesame oil
⅛ teaspoon Chinese Five Spice powder
1 piece fresh ginger root, sliced ¼ inch thick and peeled

1½ pounds turkey tenderloins

To make marinade

Combine pineapple juice, soy sauce, mustard, olive oil, honey, hoisin sauce, oyster sauce, sesame oil, Chinese Five Spice powder, and ginger root in a large nonmetal dish. Set aside.

Divide turkey tenderloins into four pieces. Using a meat mallet, pound each tenderloin until it is ½ inch thick. Place tenderloins in marinade and turn to coat both sides. Cover dish and refrigerate several hours or overnight, turning turkey at least once.

4 SERVINGS

*The peppercorn mustard has a wonderful, piquant taste that
intensifies the flavor of the turkey. Serve these colorful kebabs with
Grilled Yams and steamed julienne vegetables.*

Marinade

6 tablespoons fresh lemon juice

3 tablespoons Grey Poupon peppercorn mustard

½ tablespoon extra-virgin olive oil

¾ teaspoon freshly ground pepper

3 cloves garlic, minced

1½ pounds turkey tenderloin, cut into
  1¼-inch cubes

Kebab Vegetables

1 green pepper, cut into eight 1-inch squares

8 mushrooms

8 cherry tomatoes

1 yellow squash, cut into eight ¼-inch slices

To make marinade

Combine lemon juice, mustard, olive oil, pepper, and
garlic in a nonmetal dish. Add cubed turkey and turn
to coat pieces. Cover dish and refrigerate several hours
or overnight, turning turkey at least once.

WHEN READY TO GRILL

Alternate pieces of
turkey, pepper, mush-
rooms, tomatoes, and
squash on metal skew-
ers. Over hot coals,
place kebabs on a grill
coated with nonstick
vegetable spray. Cover
grill and cook 6 to 8
minutes, turning every
3 minutes.

250 Calories
39.6 g Protein
9.0 g Carbohydrates
6.0 g Fat
22% Calories from Fat
1.9 g Fiber
239 mg Sodium
86 mg Cholesterol

4 SERVINGS

These savory turkey tenderloins will bring a taste of Hawaii to your meal. The lemongrass imbues the sauce with a lemonlike flavor and enhances the flavor of the turkey. Serve with pineapple rice and corn bread.

Marinade

6 tablespoons fresh lime juice

1½ tablespoons soy sauce

2 cloves garlic, minced

1 piece fresh ginger root, sliced ¼ inch thick
   and peeled

1½ pounds turkey tenderloins

Lemongrass Sauce

2 stalks lemongrass*

¼ cup hoisin sauce

2 tablespoons fresh lime juice

1 tablespoon Szechwan chili sauce

½ tablespoon extra-virgin olive oil

1 teaspoon sesame oil

1 piece fresh ginger root, minced

*Lemongrass is available in Asian food stores.

278 Calories
38.8 g Protein
16.0 g Carbohydrates
6.4 g Fat
21% Calories from Fat
1.6 g Fiber
497 mg Sodium
86 mg Cholesterol

To make marinade

Combine lime juice, soy sauce, garlic, and ginger root in a large nonmetal dish. Set aside.

Divide turkey tenderloins into four pieces. Using a meat mallet, pound each tenderloin until it is slightly less than ½ inch thick. Place tenderloins in marinade and turn to coat both sides. Cover dish and refrigerate several hours or overnight, turning turkey at least once.

To make Lemongrass Sauce

Remove outer leaves of lemongrass and finely sliver the inner stalk. Combine the slivers with the hoisin sauce, lime juice, Szechwan chili sauce, olive oil, sesame oil, and ginger root and blend well. Cover dish and refrigerate until ready to use.

WHEN READY TO GRILL

Over hot coals, place turkey on a grill coated with nonstick vegetable spray. Brush each one with lemongrass sauce. Cover grill and cook 6 to 8 minutes, turning every 3 minutes, brushing with sauce.

4 SERVINGS

The lime juice, cilantro, and hot pepper imbue the turkey with the ever-so-popular southwestern flavor. Serve Sonia's Tomatillo Sauce (page 196) to accent the flavors of the turkey and add Mexican Rice on the side. Leftover rice is good reheated or stuffed in a whole wheat pita pocket with thinly sliced tomatoes and red onions.

Kebab Vegetables

4 green onions, cut into eight 2-inch lengths

1 red pepper, cut into eight pieces

1 small yellow squash, cut into eight $\frac{1}{4}$-inch slices

Marinade

6 tablespoons fresh lime juice

$\frac{1}{2}$ tablespoon extra-virgin olive oil

2 tablespoons packed chopped cilantro

1 teaspoon cumin

$\frac{1}{8}$ teaspoon *each* cayenne, oregano, thyme, salt, and freshly ground pepper

1 jalapeño, chopped*

1 garlic clove, minced

1$\frac{1}{4}$ pounds turkey tenderloin, cut into 1$\frac{1}{2}$-inch cubes

Mexican Rice

1 red pepper, quartered

$\frac{3}{4}$ cup packed cilantro

1 medium onion, peeled and quartered

3 roma tomatoes, diced

1 clove garlic, peeled

1 tablespoon extra-virgin olive oil

1$\frac{1}{2}$ cups long-grain rice

1 can (14 $\frac{1}{2}$ ounces) fat free chicken broth

$\frac{1}{4}$ teaspoon salt

$\frac{1}{8}$ teaspoon freshly ground pepper

2 dashes hot pepper sauce

*The seeds of jalapeños are very hot. To avoid burning your skin, wear rubber or latex gloves when removing the seeds. Immediately wash knife, cutting surface, and gloves when finished.

To make marinade

Combine lime juice, olive oil, cilantro, cumin, cayenne, oregano, thyme, 1/8 teaspoon salt, pepper, jalapeño, and garlic in a nonmetal dish (or a 1-gallon recloseable plastic bag). Add turkey cubes and turn to coat all over. Cover dish and refrigerate several hours or overnight.

To make Mexican Rice

In work bowl of food processor fitted with a metal blade, process red pepper, cilantro, onion, tomatoes, and garlic until chopped. Coat the bottom of a large skillet with nonstick vegetable spray and add olive oil. Place skillet over moderate heat for 1 to 2 minutes. Add red pepper mixture and cook 10 minutes, stirring occasionally. Increase heat to moderately high and add rice. Cook 3 minutes, stirring frequently. Add chicken broth, salt, pepper, and hot pepper sauce and bring to a boil. Reduce heat to low, cover, and cook 15 to 20 minutes or until liquid is absorbed. Stir the rice before serving.

WHEN READY TO GRILL

Alternate turkey (reserve marinade), green onions, red pepper, and yellow squash among four skewers. Over hot coals, place turkey kebabs on a grill coated with nonstick vegetable spray. Cover grill and cook 6 to 8 minutes, turning every 3 minutes and brushing with reserved marinade.

208 Calories
32.3 g Protein
7.4 g Carbohydrates
5.4 g Fat
23% Calories from Fat
1.3 g Fiber
142 mg Sodium
72 mg Cholesterol

---

8 SERVINGS

This is the kind of food my children like to prepare when their friends come over in the afternoon. They grill the onions, green peppers, banana peppers, and roma tomatoes in a grilling wok and place the hot dogs on the grate. The grilled vegetables along with relish, sauerkraut, and yellow mustard garnish the hot dogs and turn this everyday fare into a gourmet delight! Serve with Grilled Corn in the Husk.

WHEN READY TO SERVE
Place a hot dog in each bun and garnish each serving with grilled vegetables and favorite condiments.

8 banana peppers
1 large onion, thinly sliced
1 red pepper, thinly sliced
8 roma tomatoes, halved

8 turkey hot dogs (97% fat free)
8 whole wheat turkey buns

WHEN READY TO GRILL
Over hot coals, place banana peppers on a grill. Cover grill and cook peppers 4 minutes on each side, or until skins are charred all over. Place peppers in a plastic bag for 15 minutes. When the peppers are cool enough to handle, peel away the skin and remove the top and seeds. Cut the peppers in half and set aside.

Place onions, red pepper, and tomatoes in a grilling wok coated with nonstick vegetable spray. Cover grill and cook 10 to 12 minutes, turning vegetables every 3 minutes. During the last 8 minutes of cooking time, place the hot dogs alongside the wok on the grill and cook 8 minutes or until brown, turning frequently.

232 Calories
12.6 g Protein
34.3 g Carbohydrates
4.7 g Fat
19% Calories from Fat
4.9 g Fiber
780 mg Sodium
20 mg Cholesterol

8 SERVINGS

This is a wonderful way to prepare turkey burgers! The marinade enhances the flavor of the turkey and the toppings add crunch and color. Serve with Grilled Corn in the Husk and a fresh fruit salad.

2 cloves garlic, minced
3 pieces nonfat bread
2 pounds ground turkey tenderloin
$\frac{1}{3}$ cup pineapple juice
$\frac{1}{4}$ cup soy sauce
2 teaspoons honey
$\frac{1}{4}$ teaspoon powdered ginger

8 whole wheat hamburger buns
$\frac{1}{2}$ cup chutney
8 green pepper slices, cut $\frac{1}{4}$ inch thick
8 pineapple slices, cut $\frac{1}{4}$ inch thick
8 green onions, cut in half

In work bowl of food processor fitted with a metal blade, process garlic until finely chopped. Add bread and process until finely chopped. Combine ground turkey, bread mixture, pineapple juice, soy sauce, honey, and ginger in a small bowl and blend well. Cover dish and refrigerate several hours.

WHEN READY TO GRILL
Form turkey into eight patties. Over hot coals, place patties on a grilling grid coated with nonstick vegetable spray. Cover grill and cook 5 to 7 minutes on each side.

WHEN READY TO SERVE
Place each burger on bottom half of a hamburger bun and top with 1 tablespoon chutney, a green pepper slice, a pineapple slice, and 2 pieces of green onion that form an X on top, and the top half of the bun.

384 Calories
30.9 g Protein
49.7 g Carbohydrates
6.2 g Fat
15% Calories from Fat
4.7 g Fiber
884 mg Sodium
58 mg Cholesterol

4 SERVINGS

*These turkey kebabs are exceptionally hot and spicy, and their
hot flavor is nicely balanced by the sweetness of Cranberry Chutney
(page 40). I like to serve it with Pat's Vegetable Byriani. This recipe comes
from a friend who lived in Pakistan for several years.*

Marinade

1 cup plain nonfat yogurt

¼ cup chopped cilantro

1½ teaspoons *each* cayenne, coriander, cumin,
curry powder, and paprika

½ teaspoon garam masala

¼ teaspoon cardamom

1 tablespoon fresh lemon juice

3 cloves garlic, minced

1 piece fresh ginger root, peeled and cut
¼ inch thick

1 turkey tenderloin (1½ pounds), cut into
1½-inch cubes

Pat's Vegetable Byriani

1 tablespoon canola
oil

½ cup golden
raisins

1 Bermuda onion,
thinly sliced

½ cup slivered
almonds

1 cup long-grain
rice

2 cups water

2 carrots, thinly
sliced

½ cup frozen peas

Kebab Vegetables

4 cauliflower florets, parboiled 5 minutes

2 green onions, cut into four 2-inch lengths

1 yellow squash, cut into four ¼-inch slices

1 red pepper, cut into eight 1-inch pieces

To make marinade

Combine yogurt, cilantro, cayenne, coriander, cumin, curry, paprika, garam masala, cardamom, lemon juice, garlic, and ginger root in a nonmetal dish (or a 1-gallon reclosable plastic bag). Add cubed turkey and turn to coat pieces. Cover dish and refrigerate several hours or overnight.

To make Pat's Vegetable Byriani

Line a baking sheet with two layers of paper towels and preheat oven to 150°.

Heat oil in a large frying pan over moderate heat. Add raisins and cook 4 minutes or until raisins begin to turn brown. Transfer raisins to paper-lined pan and place in the oven. To the same frying pan, add the onions and cook over moderate to moderately high heat for 15 to 20 minutes, or until the onion slices begin to turn brown, stirring occasionally. Transfer the onions to the paper-lined pan and return it to the oven. Add the almonds to the same frying pan and cook over moderate heat for 2 minutes, or until the almonds begin to brown. Transfer the almonds to the paper-lined pan and return it to the oven.

Place rice and water in a large saucepan over moderately high heat and bring to a boil. Add carrots and peas, reduce heat to low, and cook, covered, for 20 minutes.

WHEN READY TO GRILL

Alternate pieces of turkey, cauliflower, green onion, squash, and red pepper on skewers. Over hot coals, place kebabs on a grill coated with non-stick vegetable spray. Cover grill and cook 6 to 8 minutes, turning kebabs every 3 minutes.

WHEN READY TO SERVE

Combine rice mixture and put it on a platter. Make a well in the center of the rice and fill with raisins, onions, and almonds; combine well. Makes 4 main course servings or 6 side dish servings.

236 Calories
40.1 g Protein
7.5 g Carbohydrates
4.5 g Fat
17% Calories from Fat
1.4 g Fiber
108 mg Sodium
87 mg Cholesterol

4 SERVINGS

The turkey picks up the wonderfully sweet flavor of the teriyaki marinade. Serve with grilled Pineapple Slices and lemon rice pilaf.

WHEN READY TO GRILL

Alternate pieces of turkey (reserve marinade and discard ginger root), pineapple, green onions, mushrooms, and red pepper on metal skewers. Over hot coals, place skewers on a grill coated with nonstick vegetable spray. Cover grill and cook 6 to 8 minutes, turning kebabs every 3 minutes and brushing with reserved marinade the last 6 minutes of cooking time.

292 Calories
39.9 g Protein
20.4 g Carbohydrates
4.2 g Fat
13% Calories from Fat
1.4 g Fiber
1088 mg Sodium
85 mg Cholesterol

Marinade

¼ cup tamari
2 tablespoons *each* bourbon and honey
⅛ teaspoon *each* freshly ground white pepper and crushed red pepper
1 piece fresh ginger root, peeled and cut ¼ inch thick
1 clove garlic, minced

2 turkey tenderloins (12 ounces each), cut into 1½-inch cubes

Kebab Fruit and Vegetables

8 (1-inch) cubes pineapple
4 green onions, each cut into two 2-inch lengths
8 shiitake mushrooms
1 red pepper, cut into 8 pieces

To make marinade

Combine tamari, bourbon, honey, white pepper, crushed red pepper, ginger root, and garlic in a non-metal dish (or a 1-gallon reclosable plastic bag). Add turkey and toss to coat all over. Cover dish and refrigerate several hours or overnight, turning turkey pieces at least once.

4 SERVINGS

These kebabs feature the traditional foods of Thanksgiving.
Serve with Cranberry Chutney (page 40) and steamed asparagus.

Marinade

½ cup Dijon honey mustard
1½ tablespoons white wine
2 teaspoons extra-virgin olive oil
¼ teaspoon freshly ground pepper
⅛ teaspoon salt

1½ pounds turkey tenderloin, cut into
    1½-inch cubes

Kebab Vegetables

1 sweet potato (10 ounces), pierced all over with
    a fork
8 brussel sprouts, stems removed, and parboiled
    15 minutes

To make marinade

Combine mustard, wine, olive oil, pepper, and salt in a nonmetal dish (or a 1-gallon reclosable plastic bag). Add turkey cubes and turn to coat all over. Cover dish and refrigerate several hours or overnight.

Preheat oven to 400°. Bake sweet potato 45 to 50 minutes or until tender. Cool. Remove skin and cut into 1½-inch cubes. Set aside.

WHEN READY TO GRILL
(Reserve marinade) Alternate turkey, sweet potato, and brussel sprouts onto skewers. Over hot coals, place turkey kebabs on a grill coated with nonstick vegetable spray. Cover grill and cook 6 to 8 minutes, turning kebabs every 3 minutes and brushing with reserved marinade the last 6 minutes of cooking time.

334 Calories
40.7 g Protein
17.2 g Carbohydrates
10.5 g Fat
28% Calories from Fat
2.5 g Fiber
956 mg Sodium
86 mg Cholesterol

6 SERVINGS

*The spinach, herbs, and apricot preserves add a special
flavor to these turkey burgers. They are delicious topped with
grilled onions or a combination of fresh pineapple slices, onion, and green
pepper slices. Serve with Grilled Corn in the Husk and a cold pasta salad.*

1½ pounds ground turkey
1½ cups packed fresh spinach, washed, dried,
    and cut into small pieces
1 cup minced onions
½ cup whole wheat bread crumbs
¼ cup chopped parsley
2 tablespoons apricot preserves
1 teaspoon freshly ground pepper
¼ teaspoon salt

Combine turkey, spinach, onions, bread crumbs, parsley, apricot preserves, pepper, and salt in a large bowl and blend well. Cover bowl and refrigerate several hours.

WHEN READY TO GRILL
Form turkey mixture into six patties. Over hot coals, place burgers on a grilling grid coated with nonstick vegetable spray. Cover grill and cook 9 to 11 minutes, turning burgers every 3 minutes.

255 Calories
22.1 g Protein
13.6 g Carbohydrates
12.0 g Fat
42% Calories from Fat
1.1 g Fiber
230 mg Sodium
58 mg Cholesterol

4 SERVINGS

Satay is an Indonesian specialty featuring slices of marinated chicken or beef grilled and served with a peanut dipping sauce. In this recipe using turkey instead, the marinade and dipping sauce are one and the same. Serve with Grilled Crookneck Squash and rice pilaf.

Marinade

3 cloves garlic, minced

6 tablespoons reduced-fat creamy peanut butter

3 tablespoons soy sauce

2 tablespoons fresh lime juice

1 tablespoon red Thai curry paste

2 tablespoons minced fresh basil

1½ tablespoons extra-virgin olive oil

1½ tablespoons orange marmalade

¼ teaspoon curry powder

1½ pounds turkey tenderloin, cut into
   1½-inch cubes

To make marinade

In work bowl of food processor fitted with metal blade, process garlic until finely chopped. Add peanut butter, soy sauce, lime juice, red curry paste, basil, olive oil, marmalade, and curry; process until smooth.

Transfer marinade to a nonmetal dish and add turkey cubes; toss to coat pieces. Cover dish and refrigerate several hours or overnight.

WHEN READY TO GRILL

Place turkey cubes (reserve marinade) on skewers, leaving a small amount of space between pieces. Over hot coals, place turkey on a grill coated with nonstick vegetable spray. Cover grill and cook 6 to 8 minutes, turning kebabs every 3 minutes. Serve the reserved marinade as a dipping sauce for the turkey.

419 Calories
45.1 g Protein
17.5 g Carbohydrates
18.2 g Fat
39.1% Calories from Fat
1.2 g Fiber
1069 mg Sodium
86 mg Cholesterol

4 SERVINGS

The flavor of the turkey is deliciously enhanced with this zesty marinade. Serve with Grilled Yams and steamed broccoli.

Marinade

2 tablespoons *each* tarragon vinegar, honey, and hoisin sauce

½ tablespoon *each* extra-virgin olive oil and Worcestershire sauce

1 teaspoon Dijon mustard

⅛ teaspoon *each* salt, crushed red pepper, and freshly ground pepper

1 clove garlic, minced

1½ pounds turkey tenderloin

To make marinade

Combine vinegar, honey, hoisin sauce, olive oil, Worcestershire sauce, mustard, salt, red pepper, black pepper, and garlic in a nonmetal dish. Set aside.

Divide turkey tenderloins into four pieces. Using a meat mallet, pound each tenderloin until it is slightly less than ½ inch thick. Place turkey in marinade and turn to coat both sides. Cover dish and refrigerate several hours or overnight, turning turkey at least once.

WHEN READY TO GRILL

Over hot coals, place turkey (reserve marinade) on a grill coated with nonstick vegetable spray. Cover grill and cook 6 to 8 minutes, turning turkey every 3 minutes and brushing with marinade the last 6 minutes of cooking time.

229 Calories
37.7 g Protein
6.0 g Carbohydrates
5.1 g Fat
20% Calories from Fat
0.1 g Fiber
251 mg Sodium
86 mg Cholesterol

4 SERVINGS

The intense flavor of sun-dried tomatoes enhances the taste of the yogurt marinade. The marinade pairs well with the turkey and keeps it tender and juicy during the grilling process. Serve with Tabbouleh (page 276) and Grilled Vegetable Kebabs.

Marinade

6 sun-dried tomatoes packed in oil, drained
 and minced
6 tablespoons plain nonfat yogurt
3 tablespoons Dijon mustard
¼ teaspoon *each* salt, crushed red pepper, and
 freshly ground pepper

4 turkey tenderloins (6 ounces each)

To make marinade

Combine tomatoes, yogurt, mustard, salt, crushed red pepper, and black pepper in a nonmetal dish. Set aside.

Using a meat mallet, pound each tenderloin until it is slightly less than ½ inch thick. Place turkey in marinade and turn to coat both sides. Cover dish and refrigerate several hours or overnight, turning turkey at least once.

WHEN READY TO GRILL

Over hot coals, place tenderloins on a grill coated with nonstick vegetable spray. Cover grill and cook 6 to 8 minutes, turning turkey every 3 minutes.

221 Calories
38.5 g Protein
3.6 g Carbohydrates
4.8 g Fat
20% Calories from Fat
0.6 g Fiber
310 mg Sodium
86 mg Cholesterol

8 SERVINGS

*These burgers are chock-full of good things to eat: quinoa,
brown rice, and whole grain bread. Serve on whole wheat hamburger
buns topped with lettuce, sliced tomatoes, and alfalfa sprouts.*

WHEN READY TO GRILL
Over hot coals, place turkey burgers on a grill coated with vegetable spray. Cover grill and cook 9 to 11 minutes, turning turkey every 3 minutes.

1½ cups water
¾ cup brown rice
2 cups water
1 cup quinoa*
2 pounds ground turkey
4 pieces whole grain bread, torn into small pieces
4 teaspoons Worcestershire sauce
6 tablespoons honey mustard
1 teaspoon hot pepper sauce

Bring 1½ cups water to a boil in a medium saucepan over moderately high heat. Add brown rice, cover, and cook over low heat for 20 minutes. Let cool to room temperature.

Bring 2 cups water to boil in another medium saucepan over moderately high heat. Add quinoa, cover, and cook over low heat for 20 minutes. Let cool to room temperature.

Combine ground turkey, brown rice, quinoa, bread, Worcestershire sauce, honey mustard, and hot pepper sauce in a large bowl until well combined. Form mixture into eight burgers.

*Quinoa, a high-protein grain, is available in health food stores.

334 Calories
24.2 g Protein
28.7 g Carbohydrates
13.3 g Fat
35.9% Calories from Fat
1.8 g Fiber
176 mg Sodium
57 mg Cholesterol

4 SERVINGS

The spicy yogurt marinade penetrates the turkey and not only adds flavor, but keeps it moist and juicy. Serve with Tabbouleh (page 276) and Roasted Pepper Salad.

Marinade

1 cup plain nonfat yogurt
3 tablespoons minced onion
2 cloves garlic, minced
1 piece fresh ginger root, peeled and cut
    $\frac{1}{4}$ inch thick
$\frac{1}{2}$ teaspoon coriander
$\frac{1}{8}$ teaspoon *each* salt and crushed red pepper

$1\frac{1}{2}$ pounds turkey tenderloin

To make marinade

Combine yogurt, onion, garlic, ginger root, coriander, salt, and crushed red pepper in a nonmetal dish. Set aside.

Divide turkey tenderloins into four pieces. Using a meat mallet, pound each tenderloin until it is slightly less than $\frac{1}{2}$ inch thick. Place tenderloins in marinade and turn to coat both sides. Refrigerate, covered, for several hours or overnight.

WHEN READY TO GRILL

Over hot coals, place tenderloins on a grill coated with nonstick vegetable spray. Cover grill and cook 6 to 8 minutes, turning turkey every 3 minutes.

216 Calories
39.1 g Protein
3.2 g Carbohydrates
4.1 g Fat
17% Calories from Fat
0.1 g Fiber
136 mg Sodium
87 mg Cholesterol

BEEF

6 SERVINGS

Fajitas are a very popular Tex-Mex dish. After the beef is grilled, it is served in tortillas and customarily topped with an array of condiments, most of which are high in fat. Serve this healthful version, using carefully substituted lowfat ingredients instead.

Marinade

¼ cup fresh lime juice

½ teaspoon *each* lemon pepper and garlic salt

1 beef round (1 pound), thinly sliced

1 green pepper, thinly sliced

1 medium onion, thinly sliced

6 soft flour tortillas (warmed according to package directions)

6 tablespoons fat free cheddar cheese

6 tablespoons lowfat sour cream

6 tablespoons salsa

To make marinade

Combine lime juice, lemon pepper, and garlic salt in a nonmetal dish. Add beef and blend well. Cover dish and refrigerate several hours or overnight.

WHEN READY TO GRILL

Over hot coals, place green pepper and onion slices in a grilling wok coated with nonstick vegetable spray. Cover grill and cook vegetables 10 to 12 minute, or until brown and soft, turning every 4 minutes. Remove green peppers and onions to a bowl and keep warm.

Add beef to grilling wok and cook, covered, 8 to 10 minutes, or until meat is no longer pink, turning every 4 minutes.

WHEN READY TO SERVE

Divide beef and grilled pepper and onions among six warmed tortillas. Top with one tablespoon *each* cheese, sour cream, and salsa.

262 Calories
23.6 g Protein
22.8 g Carbohydrates
8.2 g Fat
28% Calories from Fat
1.8 g Fiber
310 mg Sodium
55 mg Cholesterol

6 SERVINGS

The flavor of the beef is greatly enhanced by the Mustard Sauce.
Serve with wild rice, steamed julienne vegetables, and a tossed salad.

WHEN READY TO SERVE

Spoon 2 tablespoons of warm Mustard Sauce on individual dinner plates. Place a filet on the sauce and garnish each serving with a sprig of parsley.

Marinade

2 tablespoons Dijon mustard
1 tablespoon *each* yellow and grainy mustard
3 tablespoons tarragon vinegar
1½ tablespoons pineapple juice
1½ tablespoons extra-virgin olive oil
¼ teaspoon freshly ground white pepper

6 beef tenderloin filets (5 ounces each)
salt and pepper
parsley

To make Mustard Sauce

Combine mustards, vinegar, pineapple juice, olive oil, and white pepper in a small heavy saucepan over moderately low heat and cook until heated through, stirring occasionally. Keep warm.

WHEN READY TO GRILL

Slightly flatten beef filets and lightly sprinkle both sides with salt and pepper. Over hot coals, place filets on a grill coated with nonstick vegetable spray. Cover grill and cook 4 minutes on each side or until a meat thermometer registers 145°.

292 Calories
33.2 g Protein
2.6 g Carbohydrates
15.8 g Fat
49% Calories from Fat
0.0 g Fiber
285 mg Sodium
96 mg Cholesterol

4 SERVINGS

These hamburgers are delicious served as they are on a whole wheat bun or topped with thinly sliced tomatoes, onions, red pepper rings, and lettuce.

2 pieces nonfat bread
1½ pounds (90% lean) ground round beef
¼ cup Grey Poupon peppercorn mustard
¼ cup minced parsley
4 cloves garlic, minced
2 teaspoons Worcestershire sauce
1 teaspoon freshly ground pepper
¼ teaspoon salt

In work bowl of food processor fitted with a metal blade, process bread into fine bread crumbs. Combine bread crumbs, beef, mustard, parsley, garlic, Worcestershire sauce, pepper, and salt in a large bowl and blend well. Cover bowl and refrigerate several hours. Form beef into six patties.

WHEN READY TO GRILL
Over hot coals, place hamburgers on a grill coated with nonstick vegetable spray. Cover grill and cook 4 to 5 minutes on each side.

452 Calories
39.5 g Protein
12.0 g Carbohydrates
26.2 g Fat
52% Calories from Fat
0.6 g Fiber
763 mg Sodium
121 mg Cholesterol

4 SERVINGS

*This is a fast and delicious way to prepare beef tenderloin. The cold
Noodle Salad can be prepared while the beef is marinating, and it takes just minutes
to cook the beef on a gas grill. Serve with Sweet and Sour Cucumber Salad (page 130).*

Marinade

¼ cup tamari

2 tablespoons dry sherry

¼ cup light brown sugar

½ teaspoon sesame oil

2 teaspoons sesame seeds

1 clove garlic, minced

1 piece fresh ginger root, peeled and cut
   ⅛-inch thick

1 pound beef tenderloin, thinly sliced

Noodle Salad

2 tablespoons canola oil

1 tablespoon *each* tamari and fresh lemon juice

1 teaspoon sugar

½ teaspoon sesame oil

½ teaspoon dry mustard

⅛ teaspoon salt

4 green onions, thinly sliced

2 tablespoons sesame seeds

8 ounces dry Cantonese egg noodles

Slivered green onions

550 Calories
36.1 g Protein
51.0 g Carbohydrates
21.6 g Fat
35% Calories from Fat
3.2 g Fiber
895 mg Sodium
130 mg Cholesterol

To make marinade

Combine tamari, sherry, brown sugar, sesame oil, sesame seeds, garlic, and ginger root in a nonmetal dish. Add beef and turn to coat pieces. Cover dish and refrigerate 2 hours.

To make Noodle Salad

In work bowl of food processor fitted with a metal blade, process canola oil, tamari, lemon juice, sugar, sesame oil, dry mustard, and salt until smooth. Add green onions and process until just blended. Set aside.

Preheat oven to 350°. Place 2 tablespoons sesame seeds in a small baking pan and bake 10 to 15 minutes, or until sesame seeds are golden brown. Set aside.

Cook noodles in a large pot of boiling water for 2 to 3 minutes, or until noodles are soft, stirring frequently. Drain well. Transfer noodles to a medium sized bowl. Add tamari mixture and sesame seeds and blend well. Refrigerate, covered, until ready to serve.

WHEN READY TO GRILL

Over moderately low heat on a gas grill, place beef and marinade (remove ginger root) in a grilling wok coated with nonstick vegetable spray. Cover grill and cook 4 to 6 minutes, turning beef every 2 minutes.

WHEN READY TO SERVE

Divide the Noodle Salad among four plates and top each portion with the beef strips. Garnish with slivered green onions, if desired.

6 SERVINGS

*Marinating a sirloin steak in this wonderful combination of sauces
intensifies the flavor imparted by the grilling smoke and keeps the meat
juicy. Serve with Grilled Corn in the Husk and your favorite tossed salad.*

WHEN READY TO GRILL
Over hot coals, place steak on a grill coated with nonstick vegetable spray. Sear steak for 1 minute on each side. Cover grill and cook steak 4 to 6 minutes on each side, or until a meat thermometer registers 155 to 160°. Allow steak to sit 5 minutes before carving it into thin slices.

Marinade
¼ cup ketchup
2 tablespoons *each* white wine and soy sauce
1 tablespoon *each* balsamic vinegar and
    steak sauce
½ tablespoon *each* honey, Worcestershire sauce,
    and extra-virgin olive oil
¼ teaspoon *each* thyme and freshly
    ground pepper

1 sirloin tip steak (2¼ pounds), all visible
    fat removed

To make marinade
Combine ketchup, wine, soy sauce, vinegar, steak sauce, honey, Worcestershire sauce, olive oil, thyme, and pepper in a nonmetal dish (or a 1-gallon reclosable plastic bag). Add steak and turn to coat both sides. Cover dish and refrigerate several hours or overnight, turning steak at least once.

302 Calories
41.6 g Protein
3.0 g Carbohydrates
12.9 g Fat
38.4% Calories from Fat
0.1 g Fiber
351 mg Sodium
122 mg Cholesterol

4 SERVINGS

*The marinade is a cornucopia of flavors that helps create
an exceptionally delicious and juicy steak. Serve with mugs of
chilled Grilled Tomato Soup and a tossed salad.*

Marinade

¼ cup *each* tamari and white wine vinegar

1 tablespoon *each* extra-virgin olive oil,
    Worcestershire sauce, and fresh lemon juice

1 tablespoon dry mustard

1 teaspoon freshly ground pepper

¼ teaspoon salt

2 cloves garlic, minced

1 top loin sirloin steak (1½ pounds), all visible
    fat removed

To make marinade

Combine tamari, vinegar, olive oil, Worcestershire
sauce, lemon juice, dry mustard, pepper, salt, and garlic
in a nonmetal dish (or 1-gallon reclosable plastic bag).
Add steak and turn to coat both sides. Cover dish and
refrigerate several hours or overnight, turning steak at
least once.

WHEN READY TO GRILL

Over hot coals, place steak on a grill coated with nonstick vegetable spray. Sear steak for 1 minute on each side. Cover grill and cook 4 to 6 minutes on each side, or until a meat thermometer registers 155 to 160°. Allow steak to sit 5 minutes before carving into thin slices.

313 Calories
42.6 g Protein
2.2 g Carbohydrates
14.3 g Fat
41.2% Calories from Fat
0.0 g Fiber
678 mg Sodium
122 mg Cholesterol

6 SERVINGS

This fabulous recipe was given to me by a friend who is one of the best cooks I know. The marinade complements all cuts of beef, but I prefer to use the leaner ones. Serve with wild rice mixed with toasted pine nuts and raisins and a mixed green salad.

WHEN READY TO GRILL

Over hot coals, place beef filets on a grill coated with nonstick vegetable spray. Sear filets for 1 minute on each side. Cover grill and cook 4 minutes on each side or until a meat thermometer registers 145°.

279 Calories
32.9 g Protein
6.3 g Carbohydrates
11.0 g Fat
35.5% Calories from Fat
0.0 g Fiber
444 mg Sodium
96 mg Cholesterol

Marinade

½ cup beef or chicken stock
¼ cup *each* honey and soy sauce
½ teaspoon powdered ginger
¼ teaspoon dry mustard
½ clove garlic, minced
1 to 2 jiggers bourbon or gin

6 filets of beef tenderloin (5 ounces each),
    slightly flattened

To make marinade

Combine stock, honey, soy sauce, ginger, mustard, and garlic in a medium saucepan over moderate heat. Bring to a boil and simmer 5 minutes. Add bourbon and blend well. Remove saucepan from heat and allow the marinade to come to room temperature.

Pour marinade into a nonmetal dish (or a 1-gallon reclosable bag) and add beef; turn to coat both sides. Cover dish and refrigerate several hours or overnight, turning meat at least once.

6 SERVINGS

This is a quick and easy recipe to prepare. The marinated beef is delicious in combination with grilled onions and mushrooms and is further highlighted by the tasty whole wheat pita pockets and melted cheese. Serve with mugs of chilled soup.

Marinade
½ cup tamari
¼ cup dry white wine

1 pound beef tenderloin, thinly sliced

1 large onion, thinly sliced
½ pound mushrooms, washed and sliced
6 whole wheat pita pockets, halved
¾ cup shredded lowfat cheddar cheese

To make marinade
Combine tamari and wine in a nonmetal dish (or a 1-gallon reclosable plastic bag). Add beef and turn to coat all over. Cover dish and refrigerate several hours or overnight.

WHEN READY TO GRILL
Over hot coals, place onions and mushrooms in a grilling wok coated with nonstick vegetable spray. Cover grill and cook 10 to 12 minutes, or until vegetables are soft, turning every 4 minutes. Transfer vegetables to a bowl and keep warm.

Add beef to the same wok and cook, covered, 3 to 5 minutes, or just until beef is no longer pink, turning every minute.

Preheat oven to 400°.

WHEN READY TO SERVE
Warm pita according to package directions. Divide the meat and vegetables among the pita halves and top each with 2 tablespoons cheese. Bake 5 minutes, or until cheese melts.

328 Calories
31.4 g Protein
29.9 g Carbohydrates
8.1 g Fat
22.1% Calories from Fat
4.0 g Fiber
1742 mg Sodium
54 mg Cholesterol

4 SERVINGS

*Assembling the beef, lettuce leaves, and topping it with a variety of
condiments creates a zestfully delicious sandwich. The finished product can
be served as an appetizer or as the main course with steamed rice.*

Marinade

6 tablespoons tamari

2 tablespoons honey

1 tablespoon rice wine

1 tablespoon toasted sesame seeds*

1½ teaspoons sesame oil

⅛ teaspoon salt

1 clove garlic, minced

1 piece fresh ginger root, peeled and cut
   ¼ inch thick

1 pound beef tenderloin, sliced paper thin

24 large red leaf lettuce leaves

Condiments

4 green onions, julienned

3 cloves garlic, julienned

1 small daikon, julienned

2 small carrots, julienned

Bean sprouts

Hot bean paste

*To toast sesame seeds, place sesame seeds in a small pan and
bake in a 350° oven 15 minutes, or until golden brown.

417 Calories
35.6 g Protein
37.6 g Carbohydrates
12.6 g Fat
27.2% Calories from Fat
3.7 g Fiber
1657 mg Sodium
77 mg Cholesterol

To make marinade

Combine tamari, honey, rice wine, sesame seeds, sesame oil, salt, garlic, and ginger root in a nonmetal dish. Add beef and turn to coat pieces. Cover dish and refrigerate 3 hours.

WHEN READY TO GRILL

Over hot coals, place beef in a grilling wok coated with nonstick vegetable spray. Cover grill and cook 3 to 5 minutes, or just until beef is no longer red, stirring every 1 to 2 minutes.

WHEN READY TO SERVE

Arrange the beef and lettuce leaves on platters and the condiments in individual bowls. Allow guests or family to create their own sandwich by spreading a little hot bean paste on a lettuce leaf and placing some meat and one or all of the condiments on top. Fold the sides of the lettuce to enclose the beef and then bring the top and bottom part of the lettuce over to seal it.

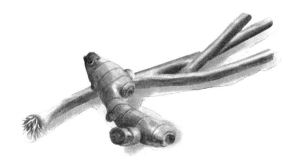

4 SERVINGS

The marinade has an Asian flavor, and it adds a wonderful essence to the London broil. It is especially flavorful and colorful with the roasted pepper slices. Serve with spaghetti squash and Grilled Vegetable Kebabs.

Marinade

2 tablespoons *each* soy sauce and rice vinegar

1 tablespoon *each* dry sherry and honey

1 tablespoon fresh lemon juice

½ teaspoon sesame oil

½ teaspoon dry mustard

¼ teaspoon crushed red pepper

2 cloves garlic, minced

1 piece fresh ginger root, peeled and cut
  ¼ inch thick

1 London broil (1½ pounds)

2 large red peppers

To make marinade

Combine soy sauce, rice vinegar, sherry, honey, lemon juice, sesame oil, mustard, crushed red pepper, garlic, and ginger root in a nonmetal dish (or a 1-gallon reclosable plastic bag). Add London broil and turn to coat both sides. Cover dish and refrigerate overnight, turning beef occasionally.

315 Calories
40.4 g Protein
7.9 g Carbohydrates
12.3 g Fat
35.2% Calories from Fat
0.3 g Fiber
749 mg Sodium
105 mg Cholesterol

WHEN READY TO GRILL

Over hot coals, place the red peppers on a grill. Cover grill and cook 14 to 20 minutes, or until skins are charred all over, turning peppers as skins blacken. Place the peppers in a plastic bag for 15 minutes. When peppers are cool enough to handle, peel away the skin and remove the top and seeds (do not rinse the peppers). Cut peppers into thin strips and set aside.

Place London broil on grill. Sear steak for 1 minute on each side. Cover grill and cook 4 to 6 minutes on each side, or until a meat thermometer registers 155 to 160°, brushing beef with marinade occasionally.

WHEN READY TO SERVE

Carve London broil into very thin slices, cutting against grain. Arrange sliced beef on individual dinner plates and garnish each serving with red pepper strips.

6 SERVINGS

*The array of colorful peppers makes this entree a beautiful presentation.
The peppers also add a robust flavor that complements the savory marinated
beef. Serve with Grilled Ratatouille and sautéed new potatoes.*

1 red pepper
1 yellow pepper
1 orange pepper

1 eye of round roast (2 pounds)

Marinade
¼ cup *each* soy sauce and red wine vinegar
2 tablespoons Worcestershire sauce
1 tablespoon dry mustard
½ tablespoon extra-virgin olive oil
¾ teaspoon freshly ground pepper
3 cloves garlic, minced

WHEN READY TO GRILL
Over hot coals, place the peppers on a grill. Cover grill and
cook 14 to 20 minutes, or until skins are charred all over,
turning peppers as skins blacken. Place peppers in a plastic bag for 15 minutes. When the peppers are cool enough
to handle, peel away the skin and remove the top and
seeds (do not rinse the peppers). Cut peppers into
quarters.

271 Calories
37.3 g Protein
6.9 g Carbohydrates
9.9 g Fat
33.0% Calories from Fat
0.9 g Fiber
817 mg Sodium
95 mg Cholesterol

Using a sharp knife, make a pocket in the roast by cutting lengthwise across the top, leaving a 1-inch uncut border on both sides, and cutting halfway down through the meat. Spoon the roasted peppers into the pocket and sew the opening shut with a poultry lacer or large needle and heavy thread. If there are peppers left over, they can be slivered and used as a garnish.

To make marinade

Combine soy sauce, vinegar, Worcestershire sauce, mustard, olive oil, pepper, and garlic in a nonmetal dish (or a 1-gallon reclosable plastic bag). Add beef roast and turn to coat both sides. Cover dish and refrigerate overnight, turning beef at least once.

WHEN READY TO GRILL

Prepare a grill with a drip pan in the center and an equal number of briquettes on each side. When the coals are hot, place the beef roast (reserve the marinade) on a grill coated with nonstick vegetable spray. Sear the roast for 2 minutes on each side. Move beef roast with tongs directly over the drip pan and cover the grill. Cook the beef roast for 40 to 45 minutes, or until a meat thermometer registers 160°, brushing with marinade occasionally. Allow the beef roast to sit 5 minutes before carving it into thin slices. Garnish each serving with any remaining peppers.

6 SERVINGS

The strong flavors of the mustard and bourbon complement the smoky flavor of the beef. Serve this savory beef entree with Roasted Potatoes (page 10) and sautéed cherry tomatoes.

Marinade

⅓ cup Grey Poupon peppercorn mustard

3 tablespoons bourbon

2 tablespoons firmly packed dark brown sugar

1 tablespoon *each* Worcestershire sauce and extra-virgin olive oil

2 cloves garlic, minced

1 beef tenderloin (2 pounds), all visible fat removed

To make marinade

Combine mustard, bourbon, brown sugar, Worcestershire sauce, olive oil, and garlic in a nonmetal dish (or a 1-gallon reclosable plastic bag). Add beef and turn to coat both sides. Cover dish and refrigerate several hours or overnight.

322 Calories
35.5 g Protein
6.3 g Carbohydrates
15.7 g Fat
43.8% Calories from Fat
0.0 g Fiber
461 mg Sodium
102 mg Cholesterol

WHEN READY TO GRILL

Prepare a grill with a drip pan in the center of the lower grate and place an equal number of briquettes on both sides of pan. When the coals are hot, place beef tenderloin (reserve marinade*) over coals on a grill coated with non-stick vegetable spray. Sear beef for 2 minutes on each side. Move the beef with tongs directly over the drip pan. Cover grill and cook 45 to 60 minutes, or until a meat thermometer registers 150°, brushing with reserved marinade occasionally. Allow the beef to sit for 5 minutes before carving into thin slices.

*The reserved marinade can be made into a sauce by combining it with 1 cup sliced mushrooms in a small heavy saucepan over moderate heat and cooking until heated through.

4 SERVINGS

*This salad is a light and refreshing meal to enjoy on a
hot summer day. The beef and dressing can be prepared ahead and the
rest of the salad combined at the last minute. Serve with cut-up fresh melons.*

Oriental Salad Dressing

1½ teaspoons chopped fresh ginger root
1 small garlic clove
½ cup rice vinegar
1 tablespoon *each* extra-virgin olive oil and tamari
1 tablespoon sugar
¼ teaspoon *each* crushed red pepper and salt

1 pound beef tenderloin, thinly sliced

Salad

3 cups sliced bok choy
2 cups bean sprouts
3 green onions, thinly sliced
1 small red pepper, thinly sliced
1 small yellow pepper, thinly sliced
1 tablespoon sesame seeds

289 Calories
30.0 g Protein
12.7 g Carbohydrates
13.6 g Fat
42.3% Calories from Fat
2.0 g Fiber
485 mg Sodium
77 mg Cholesterol

To make Oriental Salad Dressing

In work bowl of food processor fitted with a metal blade, process ginger root and garlic until chopped. Add rice vinegar, olive oil, tamari, sugar, crushed red pepper, and salt and process until blended. Transfer dressing to a covered container and refrigerate until ready to use.

WHEN READY TO GRILL

Over hot coals, place beef tenderloin in a grilling wok coated with nonstick vegetable spray. Cover grill and cook 4 to 6 minutes, or just until beef is no longer pink, turning every 2 minutes. Transfer beef to a bowl and pour 1 to 2 tablespoons Oriental Salad Dressing over beef and turn to coat all over. Refrigerate, covered, until ready to use.

WHEN READY TO SERVE

Combine bok choy, bean sprouts, onions, red and yellow peppers, sesame seeds, and beef in a large salad bowl. Add Oriental Salad Dressing and toss to blend well. Divide the salad among four dinner plates.

6 SERVINGS

This is a wonderfully quick and easy way to prepare a delicious sirloin steak. It takes almost no effort at all to create this great marinade and the taste belies its simplicity. Serve with Grilled Vegetable Kebabs and Grilled Corn in the Husk.

Marinade
¼ cup soy sauce
3 tablespoons honey
2 tablespoons rice vinegar
2 teaspoons powdered ginger
2 cloves garlic, minced
1 tablespoon extra-virgin olive oil
1 green onion, minced

1 sirloin steak (2 pounds), all visible fat removed

To make marinade
Combine soy sauce, honey, rice vinegar, ginger, garlic, olive oil, and green onion in a nonmetal dish (or a 1-gallon reclosable plastic bag). Add sirloin steak and turn to coat both sides. Cover dish and refrigerate several hours, turning steak at least once.

WHEN READY TO GRILL
Over hot coals, place steak on grill coated with nonstick vegetable spray. Sear steak for 1 minute on each side. Cover grill and cook 4 to 6 minutes on each side, or until a meat thermometer registers 155 to 160°. Allow steak to sit for 5 minutes before carving it into thin slices.

286 Calories
37.6 g Protein
5.2 g Carbohydrates
12.2 g Fat
38.4% Calories from Fat
0.1 g Fiber
421 mg Sodium
109 mg Cholesterol

6 SERVINGS

*London broil is one of the leanest cuts of beef. The marinade tenderizes
the beef overnight, so it remains very juicy and flavorful after it has been grilled.
Serve with Grilled Vegetable Kebabs and a mixed green salad.*

Marinade

½ cup Marie's Zesty Fatfree Italian Dressing

¼ cup *each* soy sauce and cider vinegar

2 tablespoons firmly packed dark brown sugar

2 cloves garlic, minced

½ teaspoon ground ginger

¼ teaspoon *each* paprika and freshly
   ground pepper

⅛ teaspoon cayenne

1 London broil (1½ pounds), all visible
   fat removed

To make marinade

Combine Italian dressing, soy sauce, cider vinegar,
brown sugar, garlic, ginger, paprika, pepper, and
cayenne in a nonmetal dish (or a 1-gallon reclosable
plastic bag). Add London broil and turn to coat both
sides. Cover dish and refrigerate overnight, turning beef
at least once.

WHEN READY TO GRILL

Over hot coals, place London broil on a grill coated with
nonstick vegetable spray. Sear beef for 1 minute on each
side. Cover grill and cook 4 to 6 minutes on each side, or
until a meat thermometer registers 155 to 160°. Allow the
London broil to sit for 5 minutes before carving it across
the grain into very thin slices.

209 Calories
26.6 g Protein
6.8 g Carbohydrates
7.7 g Fat
33.3% Calories from Fat
0.0 g Fiber
503 mg Sodium
70 mg Cholesterol

4 SERVINGS

*The fusion of the red wine, balsamic vinegar, mustard,
and spices adds a robust flavor to the steak. Serve with
Grilled Acorn Squash and Couscous and Vegetable Salad.*

Marinade
¼ cup dry red wine
2 tablespoons Dijon mustard
1 tablespoon balsamic vinegar
½ tablespoon extra-virgin olive oil
½ tablespoon *each* rosemary, sage, and oregano
½ teaspoon freshly ground pepper
¼ teaspoon salt
2 cloves garlic, minced

1 sirloin steak (1½ pounds), all visible
   fat removed

Couscous and Vegetable Salad
Dressing
1 shallot, peeled
¼ cup white wine vinegar
1 teaspoon Dijon mustard
⅛ teaspoon *each* salt and white pepper
¼ cup extra-virgin olive oil

½ cup couscous
¾ cup boiling water
½ cup *each* chopped red pepper and
   yellow squash
6 tablespoons minced Bermuda onion
¼ cup dressing

311 Calories
42.2 g Protein
1.6 g Carbohydrates
13.9 g Fat
40.1% Calories from Fat
0.1 g Fiber
259 mg Sodium
123 mg Cholesterol

To make marinade

Combine red wine, mustard, balsamic vinegar, olive oil, rosemary, sage, oregano, pepper, salt, and garlic in a nonmetal dish (or a 1-gallon reclosable plastic bag). Add sirloin and turn to coat both sides. Cover dish and refrigerate several hours or overnight, turning steak at least once.

To make Couscous and Vegetable Salad

Prepare dressing. In work bowl of food processor fitted with metal blade, process shallot until chopped. Add wine vinegar, mustard, salt, and pepper and process until blended. Add olive oil in a slow steady stream and process until well blended.

Place couscous in a medium bowl and pour boiling water over it; let sit for 15 minutes. Add red pepper, squash, and onion and blend. Add dressing and blend well. Taste for seasoning. Serve the salad immediately or cover bowl and allow to sit at room temperature for 2 to 3 hours.

WHEN READY TO GRILL

Over hot coals, place steak on grill coated with nonstick vegetable spray. Sear steak for 1 minute on each side. Cover grill and cook steak 4 to 6 minutes on each side or until a meat thermometer registers 155 to 160°. Allow steak to sit for 5 minutes before carving it into thin slices.

4 SERVINGS

This colorful salsa is a sensational combination of southwestern flavors and textures. Serve this entree with a Grilled Potato topped with lowfat or fat free sour cream and a hefty scoop of the Gazpacho Salsa.

Marinade
¼ cup fresh lime juice
1 teaspoon extra-virgin olive oil
3 cloves garlic, minced
½ teaspoon *each* cumin, cayenne, and
    chili powder
¼ teaspoon freshly ground pepper

1½ pounds top sirloin steak, all visible
    fat removed

Gazpacho Salsa
½ cup *each* diced red and yellow pepper
½ cup *each* diced red onion and tomato
2 cloves garlic, minced
2 jalapeños, seeded and diced*
2 tablespoons cilantro, finely chopped
1 tablespoon extra-virgin olive oil
½ tablespoon sherry vinegar

*The seeds of jalapeño peppers are very hot. To avoid burning your skin, wear rubber or latex gloves when removing the seeds. Immediately wash the knife, cutting surface, and gloves when finished.

359 Calories
43.3 g Protein
9.0 g Carbohydrates
16.7 g Fat
41.8% Calories from Fat
1.7 g Fiber
98 mg Sodium
123 mg Cholesterol

To make marinade
Combine lime juice, olive oil, garlic, cumin, cayenne, chili powder, and pepper in a nonmetal dish (or a 1-gallon reclosable plastic bag). Add steak and turn to coat both sides. Cover dish and refrigerate several hours or overnight, turning steak at least once.

To make Gazpacho Salsa
Combine red and yellow peppers, onions, tomatoes, garlic, jalapeños, cilantro, olive oil, and sherry vinegar in a medium bowl and blend well. Refrigerate, covered, until ready to serve. Makes 2 cups.

WHEN READY TO GRILL
Over hot coals, place steak on grill coated with nonstick vegetable spray. Sear steak for 1 minute on each side. Cover grill and cook 4 to 6 minutes on each side or until a meat thermometer registers 155 to 160°. Allow steak to sit for 5 minutes.

WHEN READY TO SERVE
Carve steak into thin slices and either spoon some of the Gazpacho Salsa over the top or place it beside the steak.

4 SERVINGS

The exotic taste combination of spices, herbs, and pineapple juice belies the simplicity of this excellent marinade. It not only imparts a rich flavor to the steak, it also keeps it moist and juicy. Serve with Grilled Polenta (page 30), string beans, and a tossed salad.

Marinade

¼ cup pineapple juice

½ tablespoon extra-virgin olive oil

1 tablespoon *each* Worcestershire sauce and steak sauce

½ teaspoon *each* dry mustard, thyme, oregano, and freshly ground pepper

⅛ teaspoon hot pepper sauce

2 cloves garlic, minced

1 sirloin tip steak (1½ pounds), all visible fat removed

To make marinade

Combine pineapple juice, olive oil, Worcestershire sauce, steak sauce, mustard, thyme, oregano, pepper, hot pepper sauce, and garlic in a nonmetal dish (or a 1-gallon reclosable plastic bag). Add steak and turn to coat both sides. Cover dish and refrigerate several hours or overnight, turning steak at least once.

WHEN READY TO GRILL

Over hot coals, place steak on a grill coated with nonstick vegetable spray. Sear steak for 1 minute on each side. Cover grill and cook 4 to 6 minutes on each side or until a meat thermometer registers 155 to 160°. Allow the steak to sit for 5 minutes before carving it into thin slices.

304 Calories
42.0 g Protein
2.2 g Carbohydrates
13.3 g Fat
39.5% Calories from Fat
0.1 g Fiber
146 mg Sodium
123 mg Cholesterol

4 SERVINGS

This dish is a kaleidoscope of colors, taste, and texture. Serve the entree
with steamed rice and pass fortune cookies and cut-up oranges for dessert.

Marinade
3 tablespoons soy sauce
1 tablespoon dry sherry
$\frac{1}{4}$ teaspoon *each* salt and freshly ground pepper

12 ounces beef tenderloin, thinly sliced

1 cup snow peas, ends removed
1 red pepper, sliced $\frac{1}{8}$ inch thick
$\frac{1}{2}$ pound shiitake mushrooms, sliced
1 tablespoon oyster sauce

To make marinade
Combine soy sauce, sherry, salt, and pepper in a non-metal dish. Add beef and toss to coat the pieces. Cover dish and refrigerate several hours.

WHEN READY TO GRILL
Over hot coals, place beef (reserve marinade) in a grilling wok coated with nonstick vegetable spray on grill. Cover grill and cook 2 minutes. Stir-fry beef for 30 seconds. Cover grill and cook 2 minutes. While beef is cooking, add snow peas, pepper, and mushrooms to reserved marinade and blend well. Remove beef to a serving dish and set aside. Add vegetables to wok and stir-fry for 1 minute. Cover grill and cook 2 minutes. Add beef and stir-fry until heated through. Transfer stir-fry to a serving dish and pour oyster sauce over top; blend well.

222 Calories
22.4 g Protein
14.6 g Carbohydrates
6.7 g Fat
27.1% Calories from Fat
2.0 g Fiber
1121 mg Sodium
57 mg Cholesterol

4 SERVINGS

*This recipe can be made with less beef and more broccoli and onions
to further reduce the fat and calories. Serve with steamed basmati rice.*

Marinade
1 tablespoon cold water
½ tablespoon soy sauce
1 teaspoon sugar
1 piece fresh ginger root, peeled and sliced
   ½ inch thick

½ pound beef tenderloin, thinly sliced

Sauce
2 tablespoons oyster sauce
½ tablespoon *each* rice wine and soy sauce
1 teaspoon sugar

2½ cups broccoli florets
8 green onions, cut into 2-inch pieces

159 Calories
18.0 g Protein
12.6 g Carbohydrates
4.6 g Fat
25.8% Calories from Fat
3.6 g Fiber
623 mg Sodium
38 mg Cholesterol

To make marinade

Combine water, soy sauce, sugar, and ginger root in a nonmetal dish. Add beef and toss to coat the pieces. Cover dish and refrigerate 1 hour.

To make sauce

Combine oyster sauce, rice wine, soy sauce, and sugar and blend well. Set aside.

Cook broccoli in a large pot of boiling water for 30 seconds. Rinse under cold water and drain well.

WHEN READY TO GRILL

Over hot coals, place beef in a grilling wok coated with nonstick vegetable spray. Cover grill and cook 2 minutes. Stir-fry beef for 30 seconds. Cover grill and cook 2 more minutes. Remove beef to a serving dish and set aside. Add broccoli and green onions to wok and stir-fry 1 minute. Cover grill and cook 2 minutes. Add beef and sauce and stir-fry until heated through.

4 SERVINGS

This Epicurean delight is a composition of Asian-flavored slivered beef and crisp green peppers and onions. Start the meal with a bowl of won ton soup and serve the entree with steamed rice.

Marinade

3 tablespoons soy sauce

2 teaspoons rice wine

$\frac{1}{2}$ teaspoon salt

1 piece fresh ginger root, peeled and sliced
$\frac{1}{4}$ inch thick

12 ounces beef tenderloin, very thinly sliced

Sauce

$1\frac{1}{2}$ tablespoons soy sauce

2 teaspoons sugar

2 green onions, cut into 2-inch pieces
2 green peppers, sliced $\frac{1}{8}$ inch thick

174 Calories
20.9 g Protein
6.9 g Carbohydrates
6.6 g Fat
34.3% Calories from Fat
0.7 g Fiber
1275 mg Sodium
58 mg Cholesterol

To make marinade

Combine 3 tablespoons soy sauce, rice wine, salt, and ginger root in a nonmetal dish. Add beef and toss to coat pieces. Cover dish and refrigerate at least 4 hours.

To make sauce

Combine 1½ tablespoons soy sauce and sugar in a small dish. Set aside.

WHEN READY TO GRILL

Over hot coals, place beef (reserve marinade and remove ginger root) in a grilling wok coated with nonstick vegetable spray on a grill. Cover grill and cook 2 minutes. Stir-fry beef for 30 seconds. Cover grill and cook 2 minutes. Remove beef to a serving dish and set aside. Add green onions and peppers to wok and cook, covered, for 3 minutes. Add beef and stir-fry until heated through. Transfer stir-fry to a serving dish and pour reserved marinade and sauce over top; blend well.

4 SERVINGS

*This is a quick and easy meal that is both colorful
and nutritious—certain to become a family favorite!*

Marinade
¼ cup sherry
1 large clove garlic, minced
1 teaspoon oregano
½ teaspoon freshly ground pepper
¼ teaspoon salt

12 ounces beef tenderloin, very thinly sliced

2 green peppers, sliced ⅛ inch thick
½ pound fresh mushrooms, thinly sliced
2 firm tomatoes, cut into 12 wedges each
4 green onions, sliced

To make marinade
Combine sherry, garlic, oregano, pepper, and salt in a nonmetal dish. Add beef and toss to coat pieces. Cover dish and refrigerate at least 4 hours.

WHEN READY TO GRILL
Over hot coals, place beef in a grilling wok coated with nonstick vegetable spray on grill. Cover grill and cook 2 minutes. Stir-fry beef for 30 seconds. Cover grill and cook 2 minutes. Remove beef to a serving dish and set aside. Add green peppers to wok and cook, covered, for 3 minutes. Add mushrooms, tomatoes, and green onions and stir-fry for 30 seconds. Cover grill and cook 2 minutes. Add beef and stir-fry until heated through.

191 Calories
21.7 g Protein
9.1 g Carbohydrates
7.1 g Fat
33.4% Calories from Fat
2.3 g Fiber
186 mg Sodium
58 mg Cholesterol

4 SERVINGS

*The Asian ingredients in the marinade enhance the flavor of this
lean steak and make it tender and juicy as well. Serve with brown basmati
rice and a combination of steamed green beans and mandarin oranges.*

Marinade

2 tablespoons *each* tamari, pineapple juice, and
rice vinegar
1 tablespoon honey Dijon mustard
$\frac{1}{4}$ teaspoon sesame oil
$\frac{1}{4}$ teaspoon crushed red pepper

1 sirloin tip steak (1$\frac{1}{2}$ pounds), all visible
fat removed

To make marinade

Combine tamari, pineapple juice, rice vinegar, honey Dijon mustard, sesame oil, and crushed red pepper in a nonmetal dish (or a 1-gallon reclosable plastic bag). Add steak and turn to coat all over. Cover dish and refrigerate several hours or overnight.

WHEN READY TO GRILL

Over hot coals, place steak on a grill coated with nonstick vegetable spray. Sear steak for 1 minute on each side. Cover grill and cook 4 to 6 minutes on each side or until a meat thermometer registers 155 to 160°. Allow the steak to sit for 5 minutes before carving it into thin slices.

311 Calories
43.0 g Protein
2.1 g Carbohydrates
13.8 g Fat
39.9% Calories from Fat
0.0 g Fiber
694 mg Sodium
123 mg Cholesterol

6 SERVINGS

The steak picks up the citrus accent of the tangerine juice and its flavor is further complemented by the tamari and honey in the marinade. Serve with Grilled Acorn Squash and a tossed salad of mixed greens, cucumbers, and tomatoes.

Marinade
½ cup fresh tangerine juice
1 tablespoon rice vinegar
2 tablespoons tamari
1½ tablespoons honey
½ tablespoon extra-virgin olive oil
¼ teaspoon freshly ground pepper

2 pounds top sirloin steak, all visible fat removed

To make marinade
Combine tangerine juice, rice vinegar, tamari, honey, olive oil, and pepper in a nonmetal dish (or a 1-gallon reclosable plastic bag). Add steak and turn to coat both sides. Cover dish and refrigerate several hours or overnight, turning steak at least once.

WHEN READY TO GRILL
Over hot coals, place steak on grill coated with nonstick vegetable spray. Sear steak for 1 minute on each side. Cover grill and cook 4 to 6 minutes on each side or until a meat thermometer registers 155 to 160°. Allow the steak to sit for 5 minutes before carving it into thin slices.

274 Calories
37.6 g Protein
3.4 g Carbohydrates
11.6 g Fat
38.2% Calories from Fat
0.0 g Fiber
252 mg Sodium
109 mg Cholesterol

4 SERVINGS

Wasabi paste (horseradish) is a very popular condiment used in Japanese cooking. It is extremely hot! Serve the London broil with orange-glazed baby carrots and a mixed green salad.

Marinade

2 tablespoons *each* soy sauce and rice vinegar

1 tablespoon *each* rice wine, fresh lemon juice, and honey

½ teaspoon *each* dry mustard and ground ginger

½ teaspoon wasabi paste

⅛ teaspoon crushed red pepper

1 London broil (1½ pounds), all visible fat removed

To make marinade

Combine soy sauce, rice vinegar, rice wine, lemon juice, honey, mustard, ginger, wasabi, and crushed red pepper in a nonmetal dish (or a 1-gallon reclosable plastic bag). Add London broil and turn to coat both sides. Cover dish and refrigerate overnight, turning beef at least once.

WHEN READY TO GRILL

Over hot coals, place London broil on a grill coated with nonstick vegetable spray. Sear the beef for 1 minute on each side. Cover grill and cook 4 to 6 minutes on each side or until a meat thermometer registers 155 to 160°. Allow the beef to sit for 5 minutes before carving it across the grain into very thin slices.

287 Calories
39.7 g Protein
3.3 g Carbohydrates
11.6 g Fat
36.4% Calories from Fat
0.0 g Fiber
350 mg Sodium
105 mg Cholesterol

4 SERVINGS

*Hearty red wine combined with the tamari and spices in the
marinade infuses the beef with a rich flavor and tenderizes it.
Serve with Grilled Potatoes and a tossed vegetable salad.*

Marinade

$\frac{1}{4}$ cup red wine

1 tablespoon tamari

$\frac{1}{2}$ tablespoon extra-virgin olive oil

$\frac{1}{4}$ teaspoon *each* salt and freshly ground pepper

$\frac{1}{8}$ teaspoon hot pepper sauce

1 clove garlic, minced

1 beef tenderloin ($1\frac{1}{2}$ pounds)

To make marinade

Combine wine, tamari, olive oil, salt, pepper, hot pepper
sauce, and garlic in a nonmetal dish (or a 1-gallon
reclosable plastic bag). Add beef tenderloin and turn
to coat both sides. Cover dish and refrigerate several
hours or overnight.

WHEN READY TO GRILL

Prepare a grill with a drip pan in the center of the lower
grate and place an equal number of briquettes on both
sides of pan. When the coals are hot, place beef tenderloin over coals on a grill coated with nonstick vegetable
spray. Sear the beef for 1 minute on each side. Move the
beef with tongs directly over the drip pan. Cover grill and
cook beef for 40 to 50 minutes, or until a meat thermometer registers 150°. Allow the beef tenderloin to sit for
5 minutes before carving it into thin slices.

297 Calories
39.2 g Protein
0.5 g Carbohydrates
13.9 g Fat
42.0% Calories from Fat
0.0 g Fiber
286 mg Sodium
115 mg Cholesterol

LAMB

8 SERVINGS

*The combination of mustard, herbs, and lemon adds a robust flavor
to the lamb. Serve with Grilled Vegetable Kebabs and fresh pasta.*

Marinade
¼ cup fresh lemon juice
3 tablespoons red wine vinegar
2 tablespoons extra-virgin olive oil
1 tablespoon Dijon mustard
1 tablespoon freshly ground pepper
1 teaspoon rosemary
½ teaspoon salt
¼ teaspoon crushed red pepper
4 cloves garlic, minced

1 leg of lamb (3 pounds), butterflied

Combine lemon juice, vinegar, olive oil, mustard, pepper, rosemary, salt, red pepper, and garlic in a large nonmetal dish (or 1-gallon reclosable plastic bag). Add lamb and turn to coat both sides. Cover dish and refrigerate several hours or overnight, turning lamb at least once.

WHEN READY TO GRILL
Over hot coals, place lamb on a grill coated with nonstick vegetable spray. Sear the lamb for 1 minute on each side. Cover grill and cook 25 to 30 minutes, or until a meat thermometer registers 150° for medium-rare or 160° for medium, turning lamb every 8 minutes. Remove lamb from grill and allow to sit 5 minutes before carving it into thin slices. Garnish each serving with roasted red and yellow pepper slices.

319 Calories
35.2 g Protein
1.2 g Carbohydrates
18.4 g Fat
52.0% Calories from Fat
0.0 g Fiber
177 mg Sodium
120 mg Cholesterol

6 SERVINGS

My mother was a fabulous cook and baker. My favorite among the dishes she used to make was Cantonese ribs. I have adapted her recipe by preparing it on the grill, and I reduced the fat by using a leg of lamb instead of ribs. Serve with steamed basmati rice and a mixed salad of baby greens and papaya slices.

Marinade

¼ cup sugar

¼ cup water

2 tablespoons *each* ketchup and soy sauce

1 teaspoon molasses

¼ teaspoon *each* salt and freshly ground pepper

1 butterflied leg of lamb (2 pounds), all visible
   fat removed

To make marinade

Combine sugar, water, ketchup, soy sauce, molasses, salt, and pepper in a nonmetal dish (or a 1-gallon reclosable bag). Add lamb and turn to coat both sides. Cover dish and refrigerate several hours or overnight, turning lamb occasionally.

WHEN READY TO GRILL

Over hot coals, place lamb (reserve marinade) on a grill coated with nonstick vegetable spray. Cover grill and cook 25 to 35 minutes, or until a meat thermometer registers 150° for medium-rare or 160° for medium, turning lamb every 5 minutes. Baste with remaining marinade the last 15 minutes of cooking time. Allow lamb to sit for 5 minutes before carving it into thin slices.

306 Calories

31.6 g Protein

10.4 g Carbohydrates

14.7 g Fat

43.3% Calories from Fat

0.1 g Fiber

565 mg Sodium

107 mg Cholesterol

8 SERVINGS

*This is one of my favorite ways to prepare a leg of lamb. The marinade is
a unique combination of honey, mustard, lemon juice, and herbs that impressively
complements the flavor of the lamb as it is grilled. I like to serve it with roasted
red pepper slices, Grilled Polenta (page 30), and a marinated vegetable salad.*

Marinade

½ cup fresh lemon juice

6 tablespoons Grey Poupon peppercorn mustard

¼ cup *each* honey and soy sauce

½ tablespoon extra-virgin olive oil

1 teaspoon *each* rosemary and freshly
    ground pepper

½ teaspoon marjoram

4 cloves garlic, minced

1 leg of lamb (3 pounds), butterflied

To make marinade

Combine lemon juice, mustard, honey, soy sauce, olive
oil, rosemary, pepper, marjoram, and garlic in a nonmetal dish (or a 1-gallon reclosable plastic bag). Add
lamb and turn to coat both sides. Cover dish and refrigerate several hours or overnight.

WHEN READY TO GRILL

Over hot coals, place lamb on a grill coated with nonstick
vegetable spray. Sear the lamb for 1 minute on each side.
Cover grill and cook 25 to 30 minutes, or until a meat thermometer registers 150° for medium-rare or 160° for
medium, turning lamb every 8 minutes. Remove lamb
from grill and allow to sit 5 minutes before carving it into
thin slices.

333 Calories
35.8 g Protein
6.1 g Carbohydrates
17.7 g Fat
47.8% Calories from Fat
0.0 g Fiber
496 mg Sodium
120 mg Cholesterol

4 SERVINGS

The flavor of the lamb is highlighted by the combination of fresh herbs in this marinade. Serve with a Greek Salad and rice pilaf mixed with raisins and toasted pine nuts.

Marinade

¼ cup *each* dry white wine and fresh lemon juice

1½ tablespoons extra-virgin olive oil

3 cloves garlic, minced

2 tablespoons *each* chopped parsley, dill, and green onions

1 teaspoon oregano

1 leg of lamb (1½ pounds), butterflied

Greek Salad

Dressing

¼ cup red wine vinegar

¾ teaspoon *each* dry mustard and oregano

¼ teaspoon *each* salt and sugar

⅛ teaspoon freshly ground pepper

½ teaspoon minced garlic

¼ teaspoon fresh lemon juice

¾ cup extra-virgin olive oil

365 Calories
35.5 g Protein
3.0 g Carbohydrates
21.7 g Fat
53.6% Calories from Fat
0.3 g Fiber
90 mg Sodium
120 mg Cholesterol

1 small head escarole, torn into bite-size pieces

1 small head romaine lettuce, torn into bite-size pieces

1 large tomato, cut into 8 wedges

1 small Spanish onion, thinly sliced

1 green pepper, thinly sliced

8 Greek olives (*kalamatas*)

8 Greek peppers (*peperoncini*)
¼ pound feta cheese, crumbled
4 anchovy filets
2 hard-boiled eggs, each cut into 4 wedges

To make marinade

Combine wine, lemon juice, olive oil, garlic, parsley, dill, green onions, and oregano in a 1-gallon reclosable plastic bag. Add lamb and turn to coat both sides. Seal the bag and place in the refrigerator for several hours or overnight, turning lamb at least once.

To make Greek Salad Dressing

Combine vinegar, mustard, oregano, salt, sugar, pepper, garlic, and lemon juice in work bowl of a food processor fitted with a metal blade and process until blended. In a slow steady stream, add olive oil and process until smooth. (The dressing can be made ahead and stored in the refrigerator in a covered container.)

Combine escarole, romaine lettuce, tomato, onion, and green pepper in a large bowl. Add enough dressing to coat the salad; toss well. Divide the salad among four salad plates and top each serving with 2 Greek olives, 2 Greek peppers, feta cheese, 1 anchovy filet, and 2 wedges of hard-boiled egg. (The lettuce, tomatoes, onions, and green peppers can be prepared a few hours ahead and stored in reclosable plastic bags in the refrigerator.)

WHEN READY TO GRILL
Over hot coals, place lamb (reserve marinade) on a grill coated with nonstick vegetable spray. Sear the lamb for 1 minute on each side. Cover grill and cook 25 to 30 minutes, or until a meat thermometer registers 150° for medium-rare or 160° for medium, turning lamb every 8 minutes. Baste with reserved marinade the last 15 minutes of cooking time. Allow lamb to sit for 5 minutes before carving it into thin slices.

8 SERVINGS

*I like to serve this savory lamb with Green Pepper Jelly,
Grilled Polenta (page 30), and Grilled Vegetable Kebabs.*

Green Pepper Jelly

3 green peppers

6 jalapeño peppers

1½ cups white distilled vinegar

6½ cups sugar

1 package (6 ounces) liquid pectin

9 drops green food coloring

Marinade

6 tablespoons extra-dry vermouth

2 tablespoons fresh lemon juice

2 tablespoons extra-virgin olive oil

2 tablespoons tarragon vinegar

2 tablespoons chopped onion

2 tablespoons minced parsley

2 cloves garlic, minced

2 teaspoons Worcestershire sauce

2 teaspoons dried basil

½ teaspoon *each* rosemary and freshly
    ground pepper

1 leg of lamb (3 pounds), butterflied

*The seeds of jalapeño peppers are very hot. To avoid burn-
ing your skin, wear rubber or latex gloves when removing the
seeds. Wash the knife, cutting surface, and gloves immediately
after finishing.

324 Calories

35.1 g Protein

1.4 g Carbohydrates

18.3 g Fat

50.8% Calories from Fat

0.1 g Fiber

93 mg Sodium

120 mg Cholesterol

To make Green Pepper Jelly

Remove the seeds from green peppers and jalapeño peppers. In work bowl of food processor fitted with a metal blade, process peppers until finely chopped. Add white vinegar and blend well. Transfer mixture to a Dutch oven and add sugar. Bring to a boil over moderate heat. Reduce heat to low and cook 3 minutes, stirring constantly.

Remove Dutch oven from heat and let sit for 1 minute. Place a sieve over another Dutch oven and strain the mixture; discard pulp. Add liquid pectin and green food coloring to green pepper liquid and blend well. Bring to a boil over moderate heat and cook 3 minutes.

Carefully pour Green Pepper Jelly into half-pint jars and seal according to manufacturer's instructions. Makes 6 to 8 jars.

To make marinade

Combine vermouth, lemon juice, olive oil, tarragon vinegar, onion, parsley, garlic, Worcestershire sauce, basil, rosemary, and pepper in a nonmetal dish (or a 1-gallon reclosable plastic bag). Add lamb and turn to coat both sides. Cover dish and refrigerate for several hours or overnight, turning at least once.

WHEN READY TO GRILL
Over hot coals, place lamb on a grill coated with nonstick vegetable spray. Sear the lamb for 1 minute on each side. Cover grill and cook 25 to 30 minutes, or until a meat thermometer registers 150° for medium-rare or 160° for medium, turning lamb every 8 minutes. Allow the lamb to sit for 5 minutes before carving it into thin slices.

4 SERVINGS

Gyro sandwiches are very popular throughout the Middle East.
The leg of lamb is often cooked on a spit and thinly sliced or ground lamb is
combined with spices, formed into meat balls, and cooked on the grill.
The sandwiches are especially delicious when topped with Yogurt Sauce.

Yogurt Sauce
¾ cup plain nonfat yogurt
5 tablespoons chopped cucumber
3 tablespoons chopped Bermuda onion
¼ teaspoon *each* garlic powder and freshly
    ground white pepper

1½ pounds ground leg of lamb
2 tablespoons oregano
1½ tablespoons *each* garlic powder and
    onion powder
¾ tablespoon freshly ground pepper
½ teaspoon thyme
¼ teaspoon salt

4 whole wheat pitas, cut in half
1 small onion, thinly sliced
1 small tomato, thinly sliced

590 Calories
43.2 g Protein
38.7 g Carbohydrates
28.6 g Fat
43.7% Calories from Fat
4.7 g Fiber
544 mg Sodium
129 mg Cholesterol

To make Yogurt Sauce

Combine yogurt, cucumber, onion, garlic powder, and white pepper in a small bowl. Cover bowl and refrigerate for several hours.

Combine lamb, oregano, 1½ tablespoons garlic powder, onion powder, pepper, thyme, and salt in a medium bowl and blend well. Make lamb into patties by forming 2 tablespoons of lamb mixture into a ball and flattening each one with your hands.

WHEN READY TO GRILL
Over hot coals, place lamb patties on a grilling grid coated with nonstick vegetable spray. Cover grill and cook 4 to 5 minutes on each side.

WHEN READY TO SERVE
Place three lamb patties into warmed pita half. Top each serving with Yogurt Sauce, sliced onions, and tomatoes.

6 SERVINGS

The fusion of Asian flavors in this highly spiced marinade permeate the lamb. Serve with Grilled Yams and a combination of sautéed julienned carrots and zucchini.

Spicy Marinade

2 tablespoons *each* hoisin sauce, oyster sauce, soy sauce, and rice wine

1 teaspoon Szechwan chili sauce

$\frac{1}{8}$ teaspoon crushed red pepper

1 piece fresh ginger root, peeled and sliced $\frac{1}{4}$ inch thick

1 tablespoon minced garlic

1 leg of lamb (2 pounds), butterflied

To make marinade

Combine hoisin sauce, oyster sauce, soy sauce, rice wine, Szechwan chili sauce, red pepper, ginger root, and garlic in a nonmetal dish (or a 1-gallon reclosable plastic bag). Add lamb and turn to coat both sides. Cover dish and refrigerate several hours or overnight, turning lamb at least once.

WHEN READY TO GRILL

Over hot coals, place lamb on a grill coated with nonstick vegetable spray. Sear the lamb for 1 minute on each side. Cover grill and cook 25 to 30 minutes, or until meat thermometer registers 150° for medium-rare or 160° for medium, turning lamb every 8 minutes. Allow the lamb to sit for 5 minutes before carving it into thin slices.

324 Calories
34.9 g Protein
9.3 g Carbohydrates
15.4 g Fat
42.8% Calories from Fat
0.5 g Fiber
1453 mg Sodium
107 mg Cholesterol

4 SERVINGS

When I am in Seattle, the first place I head for is the Pike Place Market. Among the wonderful foods to taste, there are a variety of green pepper jellies. A salesperson recently suggested brushing the jelly on lamb chops while they are cooking on the grill for a delicious way to enjoy lamb. She was right! Serve with Grilled Vegetable Kebabs and a mixed green salad.

4 shoulder lamb chops (6 ounces each), all visible
   fat removed
8 teaspoons Green Pepper Jelly (page 110)

WHEN READY TO GRILL
Over hot coals, place lamb chops on a grill coated with nonstick vegetable spray. Sear lamb chops for 1 minute on each side. Cover grill and cook 4 to 5 minutes. Turn lamb chops over and brush each one with 2 teaspoons green pepper jelly and cook another 4 to 5 minutes.

130 Calories
8.1 g Protein
7.8 g Carbohydrates
7.4 g Fat
51.1% Calories from Fat
0.1 g Fiber
25 mg Sodium
32 mg Cholesterol

6 SERVINGS

The contrast of the spicy lamb and the subtle flavor of vegetables coated with chili oil is sensational. Serve the lamb kebabs on a bed of Mediterranean Rice Pilaf and accompany it with Raita (page 124).

Marinade

1 cup plain low fat yogurt
2 cloves garlic, minced
1 tablespoon fresh lemon juice
1 teaspoon curry powder
$\frac{1}{4}$ teaspoon *each* garam masala*, salt, coriander, and powdered ginger
$\frac{1}{8}$ teaspoon crushed red pepper

1 boneless leg of lamb ($1\frac{1}{2}$ pounds), cut into $1\frac{1}{2}$-inch cubes

Kebab Vegetables

1 tablespoon chili oil
6 cauliflower florets, parboiled 5 minutes
6 new potatoes, halved and parboiled 18 minutes
2 large carrots, cut into six 2-inch chunks, parboiled 6 minutes

Mediterranean Rice Pilaf

$4\frac{1}{2}$ tablespoons light margarine
$\frac{1}{3}$ cup chopped onions
$1\frac{1}{2}$ cups long-grain rice
3 cups fatfree chicken broth
1 cup dried apricots, diced
1 cup raisins
1 tablespoon sugar
$\frac{1}{4}$ teaspoon cinnamon
$\frac{1}{4}$ cup toasted almond slivers

*Garam masala is available in most Asian food stores.

To make marinade

Combine yogurt, garlic, lemon juice, curry powder, garam masala, salt, coriander, ginger, and red pepper in a nonmetal dish (or a 1-gallon reclosable plastic bag). Add lamb and toss to coat all of the pieces. Cover dish and refrigerate for several hours or overnight.

To make Mediterranean Rice Pilaf

Melt 2 tablespoons of the margarine in a large frying pan over medium-high heat. Add onions and sauté until translucent. Add rice and cook until golden. Add chicken broth, bring to a boil, and simmer over low heat for 25 minutes.

While rice is cooking, melt the other $2\frac{1}{2}$ tablespoons margarine in large skillet over medium heat. Add apricots, raisins, and sugar and stir until evenly coated. Cook 3 to 5 minutes or until heated through, stirring frequently. Add cinnamon, almonds, and cooked rice and blend well.

WHEN READY TO GRILL
Pour chili oil into a plastic bag and add vegetables. Roll vegetables in oil to coat pieces. Alternate pieces of lamb with vegetables onto metal skewers. Over hot coals, place skewers on a grill coated with nonstick vegetable spray. Cover grill and cook 8 to 10 minutes, turning kebabs every 4 minutes.

352 Calories
28.1 g Protein
28.7 g Carbohydrates
13.6 g Fat
34.8% Calories from Fat
5.2 g Fiber
196 mg Sodium
81 mg Cholesterol

8 SERVINGS

*While combing the shelves of the Asian food store for a new flavoring sauce,
I came upon an Indonesian condiment called* kecap manis *(sweet soy sauce).
It is thicker than regular soy sauce and contributes a marvelous flavor to marinades
and other sauces. Serve these lamb kebabs with Pat's Byriani Rice (page 54).*

Marinade

½ cup kecap manis
⅓ cup minced fresh ginger root
4 cloves garlic, minced
1 tablespoon minced fresh mint
2 tablespoons stone ground mustard
2 tablespoons water
1 teaspoon sesame oil

1 boneless leg of lamb (2½ pounds), cut into
   1½-inch cubes

Kebab Vegetables and Fruit

1 large yellow pepper, cut into 16 1-inch cubes
16 shiitake mushrooms
8 green onions, each cut into 2-inch lengths
16 fresh pineapple cubes
1 large red pepper, cut into 16 1-inch cubes

344 Calories
30.8 g Protein
25.0 g Carbohydrates
15.2 g Fat
39.7% Calories from Fat
1.5 g Fiber
462 mg Sodium
100 mg Cholesterol

To make marinade

Combine kecap manis, ginger root, garlic, mint, mustard, water, and sesame oil in a large nonmetal dish (or a 1-gallon reclosable plastic bag). Add lamb cubes and turn to coat all over. Cover dish and refrigerate for several hours or overnight, turning lamb at least once.

WHEN READY TO GRILL

Alternate lamb, yellow pepper, shiitake mushrooms, green onions, pineapple, and red pepper among metal skewers. Over hot coals, place lamb kebabs on a grill coated with nonstick vegetable spray. Cook 8 to 10 minutes, turning lamb kebabs every 3 minutes.

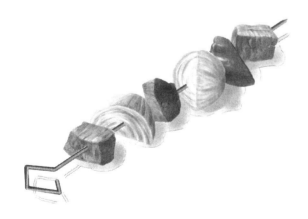

8 SERVINGS

*Shish kebabs are perfect party fare when having friends over for a barbecue.
The lemon marinade imparts a savory flavor to the lamb, which is
enhanced when grilled. While the kebabs are cooking, pass around cups of
your favorite chilled soup. Serve the entree with wild rice and a garden salad.*

Marinade
½ cup chopped onions
¼ cup fresh lemon juice
2 tablespoons extra-virgin olive oil
2 teaspoons dry mustard
2 cloves garlic, minced
¼ teaspoon *each* salt and freshly ground pepper

1 boneless leg of lamb (2½ pounds), all visible fat
    removed and cut into 1½-inch cubes

Kebab Vegetables
8 firm cherry tomatoes
8 mushroom caps
1 green pepper, cut into 8 pieces
1 red pepper, cut into 8 pieces
1 Bermuda onion, cut into 8 wedges
1 Japanese eggplant, cut ¼ inch thick

313 Calories
30.6 g Protein
7.4 g Carbohydrates
17.6 g Fat
50.5% Calories from Fat
1.5 g Fiber
142 mg Sodium
100 mg Cholesterol

To make marinade

Combine onions, lemon juice, olive oil, mustard, garlic, salt, and pepper in a nonmetal dish (or a 1-gallon reclosable plastic bag). Place lamb in dish and turn to coat pieces. Cover dish and refrigerate several hours or overnight, turning lamb at least once.

WHEN READY TO GRILL

Alternate pieces of lamb with tomatoes, mushrooms, peppers, onions, and eggplant on skewers. Over hot coals, place lamb on a grill coated with nonstick vegetable spray. Cover grill and cook 8 to 10 minutes, turning kebabs every 4 minutes.

8 SERVINGS

*The profusion of herbs, mustard, and sauces in the marinade
intensifies the flavor of the lamb. Serve with Grilled Ratatouille.*

WHEN READY TO GRILL

Over hot coals, place lamb on a grill coated with nonstick vegetable spray. Sear the lamb for 1 minute on each side. Cover grill and cook 25 to 30 minutes, or until a meat thermometer registers 150° for medium-rare and 160° for medium, turning lamb every 8 minutes. Allow lamb to sit for 5 minutes before carving it into thin slices.

329 Calories
36.0 g Protein
4.2 g Carbohydrates
17.9 g Fat
48.9% Calories from Fat
0.4 g Fiber
738 mg Sodium
120 mg Cholesterol

Marinade

½ cup *each* soy sauce and red wine vinegar
¼ cup Worcestershire sauce
¼ cup Grey Poupon peppercorn mustard
1 tablespoon extra-virgin olive oil
2 bay leaves
2 teaspoons rosemary
½ teaspoon freshly ground pepper
¼ teaspoon *each* thyme and marjoram
1 medium onion, thinly sliced
4 cloves garlic, minced

1 leg of lamb (3 pounds), butterflied

To make marinade

Combine soy sauce, vinegar, Worcestershire sauce, mustard, olive oil, bay leaves, rosemary, pepper, thyme, marjoram, onion, and garlic in a nonmetal dish (or a 1-gallon reclosable plastic bag). Add lamb and turn to coat both sides. Cover dish and refrigerate for several hours or overnight, turning lamb at least once.

4 SERVINGS

*These lamb meatballs are overflowing with the flavor of spices
and herbs. They are delicious stuffed in pita bread and
topped with grilled onions, diced tomatoes, and Raita (page 124).
Serve with Grilled Vegetable Kebabs and Tabbouleh.*

2 pounds lean ground lamb
1 cup minced cilantro
½ cup finely minced Bermuda onion
4 cloves garlic
½ teaspoon *each* cayenne, coriander, cumin,
    paprika, and freshly ground pepper
¼ teaspoon salt

4 whole wheat pita breads
1 tomato, thinly sliced
1 onion, thinly sliced
2 tablespoons Raita

In a medium bowl, combine lamb, cilantro, onion, garlic,
cayenne, coriander, cumin, paprika, pepper, and salt
and blend well. Form mixture into 12 meatballs and
place them on skewers.

WHEN READY TO GRILL
Over hot coals, place the meatballs on a grill coated with
nonstick vegetable spray. Cover grill and cook 8 to 10 minutes, turning lamb every 3 minutes.

WHEN READY TO SERVE
Prepare pita bread ac-
cording to manufac-
turer's instructions. Cut
about 1½ to 2 inches off
one side of pita to make
a pocket. Place 3 meat-
balls in each and top
with sliced tomatoes,
grilled onion slices, and
Raita.

696 Calories
52.5 g Protein
35.3 g Carbohydrates
37.3 g Fat
48.2% Calories from Fat
5.3 g Fiber
592 mg Sodium
171 mg Cholesterol

4 SERVINGS

*These spicy lamb meatballs can either be served as an
entree with rice pilaf and Raita or as a sandwich when warmed pita
bread is filled with the Koftas and topped with Raita.*

Raita

2 cups plain low fat yogurt
2 cucumbers, peeled and grated
1 medium onion, finely chopped
½ teaspoon cumin
¼ teaspoon salt

Koftas

2 slices nonfat white bread
2 tablespoons chopped onion
3 tablespoons chopped parsley
1 pound ground lamb
½ teaspoon *each* cinnamon and powdered ginger
¼ teaspoon *each* cardamom, allspice, crushed
   red pepper, salt and freshly ground pepper
⅛ teaspoon *each* mace, nutmeg, and cloves
1 medium egg

1 green pepper, cut into eight 1-inch squares
8 cherry tomatoes

443 Calories
33.7 g Protein
31.2 g Carbohydrates
20.0 g Fat
40.7% Calories from Fat
4.0 g Fiber
553 mg Sodium
141 mg Cholesterol

To make Raita

Fit a fine-sieved strainer over another strainer and place it over a large bowl. Spoon yogurt into strainer. Place grated cucumbers in a medium bowl. Allow yogurt and cucumbers to sit at room temperature for 1 hour.

Remove cucumbers from bowl and place in a strainer. Discard the liquid from the cucumbers and yogurt. Combine the yogurt, cucumber, onion, cumin, and salt in a medium bowl and blend well. Refrigerate, covered, for several hours.

To make Koftas

In work bowl of food processor fitted with metal blade, process bread into fine bread crumbs. Add onion and parsley and process until finely chopped.

In a large mixing bowl, combine lamb with bread mixture, cinnamon, ginger, cardamom, allspice, red pepper, salt, pepper, mace, nutmeg, cloves, and egg and blend well.

WHEN READY TO GRILL

Form 2 tablespoons lamb mixture into meatballs. Alternate meatballs with green pepper and tomatoes on skewers. Over hot coals, place skewers on a grill coated with nonstick vegetable spray. Cover grill, cooking 8 to 10 minutes, turning lamb frequently.

4 SERVINGS

This is a deliciously quick way to prepare lamb. It takes just minutes to combine the marinade yet the end result is a rich and succulent lamb entree. Serve with Roasted Potatoes (page 10) and grilled Turkish Eggplant Salad.

Marinade

¾ cup fresh orange juice

3 tablespoons *each* honey and tamari

½ teaspoon *each* rosemary and oregano

2 cloves garlic, minced

1 piece fresh ginger root, peeled and cut
 ¼ inch thick

1 leg of lamb (1½ pounds), all visible fat removed

To make marinade

Combine orange juice, honey, tamari, rosemary, oregano, garlic, and ginger root in a nonmetal dish (or a 1-gallon reclosable plastic bag). Add lamb and turn to coat both sides. Cover dish and refrigerate several hours or overnight, turning lamb at least once.

WHEN READY TO GRILL

Over hot coals, place lamb (reserve marinade) on a grill coated with nonstick vegetable spray. Sear the lamb for 1 minute on each side. Cover grill and cook 20 to 25 minutes, or until a meat thermometer registers 150° for medium-rare or 160° for medium, turning lamb every 8 minutes and brushing the lamb with the reserved marinade the last 6 minutes of cooking time. Allow lamb to sit for 5 minutes before carving it into thin slices.

368 Calories
35.6 g Protein
19.3 g Carbohydrates
16.0 g Fat
39.0% Calories from Fat
0.2 g Fiber
838 mg Sodium
116 mg Cholesterol

4 SERVINGS

*This leg of lamb recipe was rated number one among my tasters! The
contrast of ingredients in the marinade infuses the lamb with a wonderful taste and
makes it exceptionally moist and juicy. Serve with Green Pepper Jelly (page 110)
on the side, Zucchini and Yellow Squash Ribbons, and a mixed green salad.*

Marinade

¼ cup dry white wine
2 tablespoons *each* tamari and fresh lemon juice
1 tablespoon *each* extra-virgin olive oil, honey,
    and Dijon peppercorn mustard
1 teaspoon rosemary
¼ teaspoon crushed red pepper
1 clove garlic, minced

1 leg of lamb (1½ pounds), butterflied and all
    visible fat removed

To make marinade

Combine wine, tamari, lemon juice, olive oil, honey,
mustard, rosemary, red pepper, and garlic in a nonmetal
dish (or a 1-gallon reclosable plastic bag). Add lamb
and turn to coat both sides. Cover dish and refrigerate
several hours or overnight, turning lamb at least once.

WHEN READY TO GRILL

Over hot coals, place lamb (reserve marinade) on a grill
coated with nonstick vegetable spray. Sear the lamb for
1 minute on each side. Cover grill and cook 20 to 25 minutes, or until a meat thermometer registers 150° for
medium-rare or 160° for medium. Turn lamb every 8 minutes and brush with reserved marinade the last 6 minutes
of cooking time. Allow lamb to sit for 5 minutes before
carving it into thin slices.

364 Calories
36.3 g Protein
6.1 g Carbohydrates
20.4 g Fat
50.6% Calories from Fat
0.1 g Fiber
689 mg Sodium
120 mg Cholesterol

6 SERVINGS

*These kebabs present a beautiful array of colors and shapes and
their flavor is enhanced by the harmony of Chinese sauces and spices
in the savory marinade. The marinade can also be used with pork or poultry.
Serve this intriguing dish with steamed basmati rice and a fresh fruit salad.*

Marinade

5 tablespoons tamari

¼ cup *each* hoisin sauce, dry sherry, and honey

2 teaspoons sesame oil

1 teaspoon *each* crushed red pepper and
   dry mustard

½ teaspoon Chinese Five Spice powder

3 cloves garlic, minced

1 piece fresh ginger root, peeled and cut
   ¼ inch thick

2 pounds leg of lamb, cut into 1½-inch cubes

Kebab Fruit and Vegetables

1 starfruit,* cut into 6 slices

1 red pepper, cut into 12 pieces

3 green onions, cut into six 2-inch lengths

***The star fruit (carambola) has a smooth, waxy yellow-orange
skin with five distinct ridges. When the fruit is sliced, it resembles a star.**

346 Calories

33.6 g Protein

13.0 g Carbohydrates

16.8 g Fat

43.6% Calories from Fat

1.0 g Fiber

786 mg Sodium

107 mg Cholesterol

To make marinade

Combine tamari, hoisin sauce, sherry, honey, sesame oil, red pepper, mustard, Chinese Five Spice powder, garlic, and ginger root in a nonmetal dish (or a 1-gallon reclosable plastic bag). Add lamb cubes and toss to coat pieces. Cover dish and refrigerate several hours or overnight.

WHEN READY TO GRILL

Alternate lamb, starfruit, red pepper, and onions on skewers. Over hot coals, place skewers on a grill coated with nonstick vegetable spray. Cover grill and cook 8 to 10 minutes, turning lamb every 4 minutes.

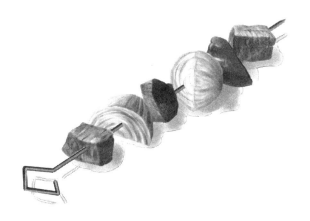

6 SERVINGS

*Thai curry pastes, found in most Asian food stores, are key
contributors to the exotic tastes of Southeast Asian food. They are a
combination of aromatic herbs, vegetables, chiles, and spices, all ground
into a paste. Yellow pastes are mild, red pastes vary in different degrees, and
green pastes are very hot. Serve this fabulous lamb with a Sweet and Sour Cucumber
Salad and mashed potatoes combined with thinly sliced caramelized Vidalia onions.*

Marinade

3 tablespoons honey

2 tablespoons *each* hoisin sauce, soy sauce,
 rice vinegar, and rice wine

1½ tablespoons curry powder

1 tablespoon red Thai curry paste

1 teaspoon sesame oil

⅛ teaspoon pepper

2 cloves garlic, minced

1 butterflied leg of lamb (2 pounds), all visible
 fat removed

Sweet and Sour Cucumber Salad

2 European cucumbers, halved lengthwise

¼ cup white wine vinegar

1 tablespoon sugar

¼ teaspoon salt

scant ½ teaspoon freshly ground pepper

301 Calories
31.9 g Protein
7.0 g Carbohydrates
15.4 g Fat
46.0% Calories from Fat
0.3 g Fiber
332 mg Sodium
107 mg Cholesterol

To make marinade

Combine honey, hoisin sauce, soy sauce, rice vinegar, rice wine, curry powder, Thai curry paste, sesame oil, pepper, and garlic in a nonmetal dish (or a 1-gallon reclosable plastic bag). Add lamb and turn to coat both sides. Cover dish and refrigerate several hours or overnight.

To make cucumber salad

Thinly slice halved cucumbers and combine with vinegar, sugar, salt, and pepper in a medium bowl; blend well. Cover dish and refrigerate several hours or overnight.

WHEN READY TO GRILL

Over hot coals, place lamb on a grill coated with nonstick vegetable spray. Sear the lamb for 1 minute on each side. Cover grill and cook lamb 25 to 30 minutes, or until a meat thermometer registers 150° for medium-rare or 160° for medium, turning lamb every 5 minutes. Allow lamb to sit for 5 minutes before carving it into thin slices.

4 SERVINGS

*This wonderful marinade enhances the flavor of lamb, and
is also good with beef. Serve with tomatoes stuffed with spinach and
a combination of wild rice mixed with toasted pine nuts and raisins.*

Marinade

2 tablespoons *each* balsamic vinegar, sweet and
    sour sauce, tamari, and dry white wine
½ tablespoon extra-virgin olive oil
1 teaspoon *each* Worcestershire sauce and
    steak sauce
½ teaspoon *each* dill weed, oregano, paprika,
    freshly ground pepper, crushed red pepper,
    rosemary, and thyme
2 cloves garlic, minced

1 leg of lamb (1½ pounds), cut into 1½-inch cubes

Kebab Vegetables

1 red pepper, cut into 8 pieces
4 mushrooms
1 small Bermuda onion, quartered

353 Calories
37.3 g Protein
8.1 g Carbohydrates
18.0 g Fat
45.9% Calories from Fat
0.9 g Fiber
381 mg Sodium
123 mg Cholesterol

To make marinade

Combine vinegar, sweet and sour sauce, tamari, wine, olive oil, Worcestershire sauce, steak sauce, dill, oregano, paprika, pepper, crushed red pepper, rosemary, thyme, and garlic in a 1-gallon reclosable plastic bag. Add lamb and turn to coat all the pieces. Refrigerate for several hours or overnight, turning lamb at least once.

WHEN READY TO GRILL

Alternate pieces of lamb, red pepper, mushrooms, and onions onto metal skewers. Over hot coals, place lamb on a grill coated with nonstick vegetable spray. Cover grill and cook 8 to 10 minutes, turning kebabs every 3 minutes.

4 SERVINGS

*Southwestern cooking is so popular today thanks to the many
wonderful restaurants, cookbooks, and cooking products of the region.
The lamb in this recipe picks up the spicy flavor of the marinade, which
is further enhanced by grilling. Start the meal with Mexican Corn Soup
and serve the kebabs with warmed tortillas and sautéed cherry tomatoes.*

WHEN READY TO GRILL

Alternate lamb, pepper, and green onions on skewers. Over hot coals, place kebabs on a grill coated with non-stick vegetable spray. Cover grill and cook 8 to 10 minutes, turning every 3 minutes.

367 Calories
38.0 g Protein
10.8 g Carbohydrates
18.8 g Fat
46.2% Calories from Fat
1.7 g Fiber
398 mg Sodium
123 mg Cholesterol

Marinade

3 tablespoons Grey Poupon peppercorn mustard
½ cup sliced onions
2 cloves garlic, minced
2 tablespoons fresh lemon juice
2 tablespoons minced cilantro
1 tablespoon white wine vinegar
½ tablespoon honey
2 dashes hot pepper sauce
½ teaspoon *each* oregano, chili powder, coriander, cumin, paprika, and freshly ground pepper

1 leg of lamb (1½ pounds), cut into 1½-inch cubes

Kebab Vegetables

1 yellow pepper, cut into eight 1-inch squares
4 green onions, cut into eight 2-inch lengths

To make marinade

Combine mustard, onion, garlic, lemon juice, cilantro, vinegar, honey, hot pepper sauce, oregano, chili, coriander, cumin, paprika, and pepper in a nonmetal dish (or a 1-gallon reclosable plastic bag). Add lamb cubes and turn to coat all of the pieces. Cover dish and refrigerate several hours or overnight.

4 SERVINGS

The yard bean, sometimes called asparagus bean,
can grow to be 2 to 3 feet in length. They add color and crunch
to this delicately marinated lamb dish. Serve with brown rice.

Marinade

2 tablespoons soy sauce

1 tablespoon dry sherry

1 teaspoon *each* red wine vinegar, hot bean
    paste*, and sesame oil

½ teaspoon honey

12 ounces leg of lamb, thinly sliced into
    1½-inch wide strips

1 pound yard beans, cut into 2-inch lengths*

4 green onions, cut into 2-inch lengths

To make marinade

Combine soy sauce, sherry, red wine vinegar, hot bean
paste, sesame oil, and honey in a nonmetal dish (or
a 1-gallon reclosable plastic bag). Add lamb and turn
to coat pieces. Cover dish and refrigerate for several hours.

    Place beans in a large pot of salted boiling water and
cook 3 minutes. Drain well and set aside.

***Hot bean paste and yard beans are available at most Asian
food stores.**

WHEN READY TO GRILL

Over hot coals, place lamb (reserve mari-nade) in a grilling wok coated with nonstick vegetable spray on a grill. Stir-fry 1 minute. Cover grill and cook 2 minutes. Remove cover and stir-fry lamb 1 minute. Add beans and green onions and stir-fry 1 minute. Cover grill and cook 2 minutes. Re-move cover and stir-fry 2 minutes. Transfer stir-fry to a serving dish and add reserved mari-nade; blend well.

222 Calories
20.9 g Protein
12.1 g Carbohydrates
9.5 g Fat
38.5% Calories from Fat
2.1 g Fiber
564 mg Sodium
60 mg Cholesterol

4 SERVINGS

*The Asian marinade and smoky flavor from the grill combine to
make a sensational, highly spiced and flavorful lamb and
vegetable stir-fry. Serve with steamed basmati rice.*

Marinade

2 tablespoons *each* hoisin sauce, water, and
  plum sauce
1 tablespoon *each* rice wine, soy sauce, Szechwan
  chili sauce, and honey
1 piece fresh ginger root, peeled and cut
  ¼ inch thick
1 tablespoon minced garlic

1 boneless leg of lamb (1 pound), thinly sliced
  into 1-inch strips

1½ cups broccoli florets, parboiled 1 minute
1 red pepper, cut into ⅛-inch strips
1 yellow pepper, cut into ⅛-inch strips
½ cup shiitake mushrooms, sliced
4 green onions, cut into 2-inch lengths

323 Calories
27.8 g Protein
24.5 g Carbohydrates
11.6 g Fat
32.3% Calories from Fat
3.5 g Fiber
583 mg Sodium
80 mg Cholesterol

To make marinade

Combine hoisin sauce, water, plum sauce, rice wine, soy sauce, Szechwan chili sauce, honey, ginger root, and garlic in a nonmetal dish (or a 1-gallon reclosable plastic bag). Add lamb and turn to coat all over. Cover dish and refrigerate for several hours or overnight, turning lamb at least once.

WHEN READY TO GRILL

Over hot coals, place lamb (reserve marinade and discard ginger root) in a grilling wok coated with nonstick vegetable spray on a grill. Stir-fry lamb for 1 minute. Cover grill and cook 2 minutes. Remove cover and stir-fry lamb 1 minute. Add broccoli, red and yellow peppers, shiitake mushrooms, and green onions; stir-fry 1 minute. Cover grill and cook 2 minutes. Transfer lamb and vegetables to a large serving bowl and add reserved marinade; blend well.

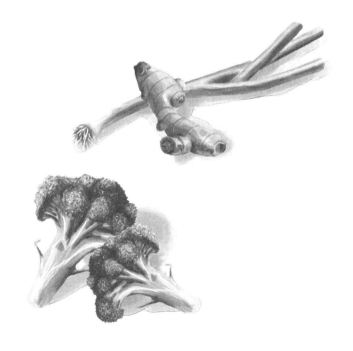

6 SERVINGS

The Iowa City Press Citizen *had a wonderful article on the joy of grilling. Wine-Basted Lamb Kebabs was a featured recipe, and it comes from the people who know everything about lamb, the Benton and Iowa County, Iowa, Sheep Producers Association.*

WHEN READY TO GRILL
Over hot coals, place kebabs 4 inches from heat for 8 to 10 minutes, turning frequently. Brush with sauce in the final minutes of cooking.

1½ pounds leg of lamb, cut into 1-inch cubes
24 Chinese pea pods
24 cherry tomatoes
24 pineapple chunks
½ cup chili sauce
½ cup brown sugar
½ cup red wine
2 tablespoons lemon juice
1 tablespoon dry mustard
½ teaspoon salt

Thread 12 skewers with a lamb cube, pea pod, cherry tomato, and pineapple. Repeat, ending with lamb.

In small saucepan, combine chili sauce, brown sugar, red wine, lemon juice, mustard, and salt. Bring to a boil, stirring until smooth. Remove from heat.

379 Calories
26.3 g Protein
39.3 g Carbohydrates
12.0 g Fat
28.5% Calories from Fat
3.3 g Fiber
524 mg Sodium
80 mg Cholesterol

PORK

4 SERVINGS

This is a delicious way to prepare pork chops. It is quick and easy and is certain to be a favorite among the younger set! Serve with Grilled Corn in the Husk.

Barbecue Sauce
¼ cup barbecue sauce
3 tablespoons peach jam
2 tablespoons horseradish
½ tablespoon Dijon mustard

4 butterfly pork chops (6 ounces each), cut
   ¾ inch thick

To make Barbecue Sauce
Combine barbecue sauce, peach jam, horseradish, and mustard in a small bowl.

WHEN READY TO GRILL
Over hot coals, place pork chops on a grill coated with nonstick vegetable spray. Sear pork chops for 1 minute on each side. Brush pork chops with half of the sauce and cook 4 to 5 minutes. Turn pork chops over and brush with remaining sauce; cook 4 to 5 minutes or until a meat thermometer registers 155°.

369 Calories
42.2 g Protein
15.7 g Carbohydrates
14.3 g Fat
34.8% Calories from Fat
0.2 g Fiber
407 mg Sodium
129 mg Cholesterol

6 SERVINGS

*The Asian flavors in the marinade and smoky taste from the grill blend
well with pork. Serve with Fruit Kebabs and steamed pea pods.*

Marinade
¼ cup tamari
3 tablespoons rice wine
2 tablespoons *each* rice vinegar and honey
1 tablespoon kecap manis*
2 cloves garlic, minced
⅛ teaspoon Chinese Five Spice powder

1 pork tenderloin (2¼ pounds), all visible
fat removed

To make marinade
Combine tamari, rice wine, rice vinegar, honey, kecap
manis, garlic, and Chinese Five Spice powder in a nonmetal dish (or a 1-gallon reclosable plastic bag). Add
pork tenderloin and turn to coat both sides. Cover dish
and refrigerate several hours or overnight, turning pork
at least once.

WHEN READY TO GRILL
Over hot coals, place pork tenderloin (reserve marinade)
on a grill coated with nonstick vegetable spray. Sear the
pork for 1 minute on each side. Cover grill and cook 15 to
18 minutes, or until a meat thermometer registers 150 to
155°, turning pork every 5 minutes and basting with marinade the last 6 minutes of cooking time. Allow pork to sit
for 5 minutes before carving it into thin slices.

***Kecap manis is an Indonesian condiment found in most Asian
food stores.**

222 Calories
34.0 g Protein
6.8 g Carbohydrates
5.6 g Fat
22.6% Calories from Fat
0.0 g Fiber
465 mg Sodium
107 mg Cholesterol

4 SERVINGS

The fabulous balance of the kecap manis (sweet soy sauce) and honey with the garlic and crushed red pepper in this marinade elevates pork tenderloin to a gourmet experience. The marinade would also enhance the flavor of lamb or chicken. Serve with Pat's Byriani Rice (page 54) and Fruit Kebabs.

Marinade
¼ cup *each* honey mustard and kecap manis*
1 tablespoon rice vinegar
2 large cloves garlic, minced
⅛ teaspoon crushed red pepper

1 pork tenderloin (1½ pounds)

To make marinade
Combine honey mustard, kecap manis, rice vinegar, garlic, and red pepper in a nonmetal dish (or a 1-gallon reclosable plastic bag). Add pork tenderloin and turn to coat all over. Cover dish and refrigerate several hours or overnight.

WHEN READY TO GRILL
Prepare a grill with a drip pan in the center of the lower grate and place an equal number of briquettes on both sides of pan. When coals are hot, place pork (reserve marinade) directly over drip pan and cook, covered, 20 to 25 minutes, or until a meat thermometer registers 150° to 155°, turning pork occasionally and brushing with reserved marinade the last 10 minutes of cooking time. Allow pork to sit for 5 minutes before carving it into thin slices.

*Kecap manis is an Indonesian condiment available in most Asian food stores.

234 Calories
33.5 g Protein
14.0 g Carbohydrates
5.8 g Fat
22.4% Calories from Fat
0.0 g Fiber
427 mg Sodium
107 mg Cholesterol

6 SERVINGS

Not only do these pork chops taste delicious, but the flavorful sauce spooned over each one is appealing to the eye. Serve with Grilled Polenta (page 30) and a salad tossed with Raspberry Vinaigrette (page 12).

Marinade

¾ cup soy sauce

1 cup pineapple juice

½ cup currant jelly

¼ cup honey

2 tablespoons *each* Dijon mustard and fresh
   lemon juice

¼ teaspoon Worcestershire sauce

1 piece fresh ginger root, peeled and cut
   ¼ inch thick

2 cloves garlic, minced

6 pork top loin chops (6 ounces each), cut
   ¾ inch thick

412 Calories
37.0 g Protein
38.3 g Carbohydrates
12.0 g Fat
26.3% Calories from Fat
0.1 g Fiber
2283 mg Sodium
107 mg Cholesterol

To make marinade

Combine soy sauce, pineapple juice, jelly, honey, mustard, lemon juice, Worcestershire sauce, ginger root, and garlic in a measuring pitcher and blend well. Pour half of the marinade in a nonmetal dish. Add pork chops and turn to coat both sides. Cover dish and refrigerate several hours or overnight, turning pork chops at least once. Refrigerate remaining marinade in a covered container to use as a sauce for the cooked pork chops.

WHEN READY TO GRILL

Over hot coals, place pork chops on a grill coated with nonstick vegetable spray. Sear pork chops for 1 minute on each side. Cover grill and cook 4 to 5 minutes on each side or until a meat thermometer registers 155°.

While the pork chops are cooking, heat the reserved marinade in a small saucepan over moderate heat. Bring to a boil and cook over moderately high heat for 12 to 14 minutes, or until sauce is reduced to 3/4 cup. Remove ginger root. Keep sauce warm over very low heat.

WHEN READY TO SERVE

Spoon 2 tablespoons sauce over top of each pork chop and garnish with a fresh sprig of parsley.

4 SERVINGS

This is an exceptional pork roast! The flavor of the marinade, laced throughout the pork, is enhanced by cooking on the grill. Serve Lemon and Egg Soup as a first course and accompany the pork with a Greek Salad (page 108) and rice pilaf.

Marinade

¼ cup white wine vinegar
1 tablespoon *each* honey and Dijon mustard
½ tablespoon extra-virgin olive oil
1 teaspoon *each* coriander and freshly
    ground pepper
¼ teaspoon salt
2 bay leaves

1 boneless loin pork roast (1½ pounds)

Lemon and Egg Soup

4 cups chicken broth
½ teaspoon salt
¼ teaspoon freshly ground lemon pepper
¼ cup rice
2 eggs
¼ cup fresh lemon juice
Chopped chives or parsley, for garnish

415 Calories
34.4 g Protein
6.0 g Carbohydrates
27.7 g Fat
60.1% Calories from Fat
0.1 g Fiber
317 mg Sodium
91 mg Cholesterol

To make marinade

Combine vinegar, honey, mustard, olive oil, coriander, pepper, salt, and bay leaves in a nonmetal dish (or a 1-gallon reclosable plastic bag). Add pork roast and turn to coat both sides. Cover dish and refrigerate several hours or overnight, turning pork at least once.

WHEN READY TO GRILL

Over hot coals, place pork roast (reserve marinade and discard bay leaves) on a grill coated with nonstick vegetable spray. Sear the pork for 1 minute on each side. Cover grill and cook 18 to 22 minutes, or until a meat thermometer registers 150 to 155°, turning pork every 5 minutes and brushing with reserved marinade after pork has cooked for 12 minutes. Allow pork to sit for 5 minutes before carving it into thin slices.

To make Lemon and Egg Soup

While the pork is cooking, combine chicken broth, salt, and lemon pepper in a medium saucepan over moderate heat and bring to a boil. Add rice, cover, and reduce heat to low. Simmer 20 minutes or until the rice is tender.

Combine eggs and lemon juice in a small bowl. On low heat, gradually add egg mixture to soup, stirring constantly. Do not let the soup come to a boil or the eggs will curdle. Ladle soup into individual bowls and garnish each serving with chives or parsley.

4 SERVINGS

*This smoke-flavored pork tenderloin is delicious accompanied
by Cranberry Chutney (page 40), Grilled Acorn Squash,
and a salad of mixed greens tossed with a raspberry vinaigrette.*

Marinade

2 tablespoons bourbon

1 tablespoon molasses

1 tablespoon *each* fresh lemon juice and
    extra-virgin olive oil

3 cloves garlic, minced

1 teaspoon thyme

½ teaspoon crushed red pepper

1 pork tenderloin (1½ pounds), all visible
    fat removed

302 Calories
33.5 g Protein
3.9 g Carbohydrates
9.0 g Fat
26.7% Calories from Fat
0.1 g Fiber
84 mg Sodium
107 mg Cholesterol

To make marinade

Combine bourbon, molasses, lemon juice, olive oil, garlic, thyme, and red pepper in a nonmetal dish (or a 1-gallon reclosable plastic bag). Add pork and turn to coat both sides. Cover dish and refrigerate several hours or overnight, turning pork at least once.

WHEN READY TO GRILL

While briquettes are getting hot, soak 1 cup smoking wood chips according to package instructions. When the coals are ready, sprinkle the wet chips over them. Place the pork tenderloin (reserve marinade) over the hot coals and sear it for 1 minute on each side. Cover grill and cook 15 to 18 minutes or until a meat thermometer registers 150 to 155°, turning pork every 5 minutes and brushing with reserved marinade the last 6 minutes of cooking time. Allow pork tenderloin to sit for 5 minutes before carving it into thin slices.

4 SERVINGS

Hot and spicy flavors of the Southwest are infused throughout the pork. Sonia's Tomatillo Salsa (page 196) on the side is a nice addition to this meal. The pork tenderloin is grilled using the indirect method, which keeps it moist and juicy. Start the dinner by serving a fabulous tortilla soup (the star attraction at a Gourmet Club dinner my husband and I participated in). The soup recipe has been slightly altered to make it lowfat.

Marinade

6 tablespoons fresh lime juice

1 tablespoon extra-virgin olive oil

1 teaspoon *each* cumin, oregano, freshly
   ground pepper, and thyme

¼ teaspoon salt

¼ cup packed chopped cilantro

4 serranos, quartered and seeded*

1 pork tenderloin (1½ pounds), all visible
   fat removed

Mary's Tortilla Soup

1 onion, chopped

1 can (4 ounces) diced green chiles

3 cloves garlic, minced

2 tablespoons extra-virgin olive oil

1 can (10½ ounces) beef broth

1 can (10½ ounces) chicken broth

1½ cups tomato juice

234 Calories
33.6 g Protein
3.2 g Carbohydrates
9.2 g Fat
35.4% Calories from Fat
0.2 g Fiber
214 mg Sodium
107 mg Cholesterol

*The seeds of serrano peppers are very hot. To avoid burning your skin, wear rubber or latex gloves when removing the seeds. Immediately wash the knife, cutting surface, and gloves when finished.

1½ cups water

1½ teaspoons chili powder

1 teaspoon cumin

½ teaspoon salt

⅛ teaspoon freshly ground pepper

1½ teaspoons steak sauce

1 teaspoon Worcestershire sauce

1 large tomato, diced

1½ tablespoons minced fresh cilantro

1½ cups oven-roasted or baked lowfat
   tortilla chips*

½ cup lowfat shredded cheddar cheese

To make marinade

Combine lime juice, olive oil, cumin, oregano, pepper, thyme, salt, cilantro, and serranos in a nonmetal dish (or a reclosable plastic bag). Add pork tenderloin and turn to coat both sides. Cover dish and refrigerate several hours or overnight, turning pork at least once.

To make Mary's Tortilla Soup

In a 2-quart kettle, sauté onion, chiles, and garlic in olive oil over moderate heat for 3 to 4 minutes, stirring frequently. Add beef broth, chicken broth, tomato juice, water, chili powder, cumin, salt, pepper, steak sauce, Worcestershire sauce, tomato, and cilantro; blend well. Bring to a boil over moderately high heat, reduce heat and simmer, covered, for 1½ hours. (The soup may be refrigerated after it comes to room temperature.)

*The original soup recipe called for making your own tortilla chips by stacking six (6-inch) corn tortillas together and trimming the sides to make a square. Cut the square into 1½ × 1-inch strips and fry them in 1 inch of vegetable oil for 1 to 2 minutes or until light brown, stirring frequently. Remove from oil with a slotted spoon and drain on a paper towel. Lightly salt while still warm. (Can be prepared ahead and stored in an airtight container.)

WHEN READY TO GRILL

Place a drip pan in the center of the lower grate and place an equal number of briquettes on both sides. When coals are hot, place the pork (reserve marinade and discard serrano peppers) over the coals on a grill coated with nonstick vegetable spray. Sear the pork for 1 minute on each side. Move the pork directly over the drip pan. Cover grill and cook 40 to 50 minutes, or until a meat thermometer registers 150 to 155°, turning pork every 20 minutes and brushing with reserved marinade. Allow pork to sit for 5 minutes before carving it into thin slices.

TO SERVE TORTILLA SOUP

If the soup has been refrigerated, reheat until hot. Divide tortilla chips and cheese among four soup bowls and pour the soup on top; serve at once.

6 SERVINGS

This is a superb company dish. The combination of grilled pork complemented by the Raisin Wine Sauce is delicious and makes a beautiful presentation as well. Serve with orange-glazed carrots and rice pilaf.

Marinade

1 cup balsamic vinegar
1 tablespoon chopped fresh rosemary
4 cloves garlic, minced
1 teaspoon freshly ground pepper

1 top loin pork roast (2 pounds), all visible
   fat removed

Raisin Wine Sauce

$\frac{1}{4}$ cup sugar
3 tablespoons cornstarch
1 teaspoon dry mustard
1 cup dry red wine
$\frac{1}{2}$ cup water
$\frac{1}{4}$ cup raisins
1 jar (10 ounces) red currant jelly

381 Calories
30.5 g Protein
27.8 g Carbohydrates
14.7 g Fat
34.8% Calories from Fat
0.2 g Fiber
85 mg Sodium
81 mg Cholesterol

To make marinade

Combine vinegar, rosemary, garlic, and pepper in a non-metal dish (or a 1-gallon reclosable plastic bag). Add pork roast and turn to coat both sides. Cover dish and refrigerate several hours or overnight, turning pork at least once.

WHEN READY TO GRILL

Over hot coals, place pork roast on a grill coated with non-stick vegetable spray. Cover grill and cook 40 to 45 minutes, or until a meat thermometer registers 145 to 155°, turning pork every 5 minutes.

To make Raisin Wine Sauce

While the pork is cooking, combine sugar, cornstarch, and dry mustard in a medium saucepan over moderately low heat. Add wine, water, and raisins and cook 5 minutes, stirring occasionally. Add red currant jelly and cook until jelly melts, stirring occasionally. Increase heat to moderate and cook 5 to 10 minutes or until sauce thickens. The recipe makes 2 cups and can be easily cut in half.

WHEN READY TO SERVE

Carve pork into thin slices and divide among six dinner plates. Top each serving with Raisin Wine Sauce.

4 SERVINGS

The simplicity of pork roast is impressively transformed into a gourmet treat by the exotic flavors in the marinade, further complemented by the unusual combination of pineapple, apples, and fresh ginger in the sauce. Serve with sautéed new potatoes.

Marinade

¼ cup hoisin sauce

1 teaspoon *each* teriyaki sauce and rice wine

1 teaspoon minced garlic

1 piece fresh ginger root, peeled and cut
   ¼ inch thick

1 boneless loin pork roast (1½ pounds), all visible
   fat removed

Ginger-Pineapple Sauce

1½ cups fresh pineapple, cubed

2 Delicious apples, peeled, seeded, and cubed

¼ cup sugar

½ cup water

1 tablespoon fresh lemon juice

½ ounce fresh ginger root, peeled and cut
   into sticks

1 3-inch cinnamon stick

350 Calories
35.6 g Protein
11.6 g Carbohydrates
17.1 g Fat
44.0% Calories from Fat
0.9 g Fiber
536 mg Sodium
91 mg Cholesterol

To make marinade

Combine hoisin sauce, teriyaki sauce, rice wine, garlic, and ginger root in a nonmetal dish (or a 1-gallon reclosable plastic bag). Add pork roast and turn to coat both sides. Cover dish and refrigerate several hours or overnight, turning pork at least once.

To make Ginger-Pineapple Sauce

Combine pineapple, apples, sugar, water, lemon juice, ginger root, and cinnamon stick in a medium saucepan over moderate heat and bring to a boil. Reduce heat, cover, and simmer 20 minutes. Remove cinnamon and ginger. Transfer sauce to work bowl of food processor fitted with a metal blade and puree. Spoon sauce into covered container and refrigerate several hours or overnight.

WHEN READY TO GRILL

Over hot coals, place pork roast on a grill coated with nonstick vegetable spray. Sear the pork roast for 1 minute on each side. Cover grill and cook 40 to 45 minutes, or until a meat thermometer registers 150 to 155°, turning pork every 5 minutes. Allow pork roast to sit for 5 minutes before carving it into thin slices.

WHEN READY TO SERVE

Divide the pork among four dinner plates. Accompany each serving with Ginger-Pineapple Sauce on the side.

6 SERVINGS

The sweetness of pineapple juice and the tanginess of orange marmalade blend into a sensational marinade—the end result is a very moist and flavorful pork chop. Serve with Tangy Applesauce (page 170) or topped with Caramelized Onions (page 166).

Marinade

¼ cup *each* pineapple juice and
   orange marmalade
1 tablespoon white wine vinegar
1 tablespoon Grey Poupon peppercorn mustard
½ tablespoon Worcestershire sauce
1 teaspoon dried rosemary
¼ teaspoon freshly ground pepper

6 loin pork chops (6 ounces each), cut
   ¾ inch thick

To make marinade

In work bowl of food processor fitted with metal blade, combine pineapple juice, orange marmalade, vinegar, mustard, Worcestershire sauce, rosemary, and pepper and process until smooth. Place pork chops in a non-metal dish and pour marinade over the top. Cover dish and refrigerate several hours or overnight, turning pork at least once.

WHEN READY TO GRILL

Over hot coals, place pork chops on a grill coated with nonstick vegetable spray. Sear the pork chops for 1 minute on each side. Cover grill and cook 4 to 5 minutes on each side or until a meat thermometer registers 155°.

273 Calories
34.7 g Protein
5.0 g Carbohydrates
11.5 g Fat
37.9% Calories from Fat
0.0 g Fiber
122 mg Sodium
107 mg Cholesterol

4 SERVINGS

The flavor of the marinade permeating the pork chops is intensified by grilling. The marinade can also be used to marinate pork or beef tenderloins, lamb, or poultry. Serve with grilled Apple Rings and steamed brown basmati rice.

Marinade

2 tablespoons *each* tamari and black vinegar*
1 tablespoon firmly packed dark brown sugar
1 tablespoon rice wine
½ teaspoon chili oil
¼ teaspoon dry mustard
⅛ teaspoon Chinese Five Spice powder
2 cloves garlic, minced
1 piece fresh ginger root, peeled and cut
    ¼ inch thick

4 top loin pork chops (6 ounces each), cut
    ¾ inch thick

To make marinade

Combine tamari, black vinegar, brown sugar, rice wine, chili oil, mustard, Chinese Five Spice, garlic, and ginger root in a nonmetal dish. Place pork chops in dish and turn to coat both sides. Cover dish and refrigerate several hours or overnight, turning pork chops at least once.

Tamari, black vinegar, rice wine, chili oil, and Chinese Five Spice powder are available in most Asian food stores.

WHEN READY TO GRILL

Over hot coals, place pork chops on a grill coated with nonstick vegetable spray. Sear the pork chops for 1 minute on each side. Cover grill and cook 4 to 5 minutes on each side or until a meat thermometer registers 155°.

339 Calories
43.0 g Protein
6.3 g Carbohydrates
14.3 g Fat
38.0% Calories from Fat
0.0 g Fiber
606 mg Sodium
129 mg Cholesterol

4 SERVINGS

*This is a colorful entree that lends itself to any combination of fruits
and vegetables; I prefer to use prunes, mango, and green pepper.
Serve with Grilled Acorn Squash and grilled Pineapple Rings.*

WHEN READY TO GRILL

Alternate pieces of pork, prunes, mango, and green pepper on skewers (reserve marinade). Over hot coals, place skewers on a grill coated with nonstick vegetable spray. Cover grill, cooking 8 to 9 minutes, turning skewers every 4 minutes and brushing with reserved marinade.

366 Calories
25.3 g Protein
39.3 g Carbohydrates
7.9 g Fat
19.3% Calories from Fat
3.0 g Fiber
1139 mg Sodium
72 mg Cholesterol

Marinade

¼ cup rice vinegar

3 tablespoons *each* soy sauce, hoisin sauce, and
    rice wine

1 tablespoon extra-virgin olive oil

1 teaspoon hot bean paste

2 cloves garlic, minced

1 piece fresh ginger root, peeled and cut
    ¼ inch thick

1 pound pork tenderloin, cut into 1½-inch cubes

Kebab Fruits and Vegetable

8 bite-size prunes

1 mango, peeled and cut into 4 pieces

1 green pepper, cut into 4 pieces

To make marinade

Combine rice vinegar, soy sauce, hoisin sauce, rice wine, olive oil, bean paste, garlic, and ginger root in a nonmetal dish (or a 1-gallon reclosable plastic bag). Add pork cubes and turn to coat. Cover dish and refrigerate overnight.

4 SERVINGS

The exotic flavors of the Pacific Rim impart a piquant taste to these delicious pork chops. Serve with steamed broccoli and grilled Pineapple Rings.

Marinade
½ cup hoisin sauce
1 tablespoon *each* miso*, soy sauce, Szechwan chili sauce, rice wine, and honey
2 teaspoons powdered ginger
1 teaspoon Chinese Five Spice powder

4 pork loin chops (6 ounces each), cut ¾ inch thick

To make marinade
Combine hoisin sauce, miso, soy sauce, Szechwan chili sauce, rice wine, honey, ginger, and Chinese Five Spice powder in a nonmetal dish and blend well. Add pork chops and turn to coat. Cover dish and refrigerate several hours or overnight, turning pork chops at least once.

*Miso, Chinese Five Spice powder, and Szechwan chili sauce are available in Asian food stores.

WHEN READY TO GRILL
Over hot coals, place pork chops on grill coated with nonstick vegetable spray. Sear the pork chops for 1 minute on each side. Cover grill and cook 4 to 5 minutes on each side or until a meat thermometer registers 155°.

311 Calories
36.5 g Protein
10.5 g Carbohydrates
12.1 g Fat
35.0% Calories from Fat
0.7 g Fiber
739 mg Sodium
107 mg Cholesterol

4 SERVINGS

Pork tenderloin is delicious grilled and covered in a rich barbecue sauce. You can use any kind of barbecue sauce, but I prefer my own recipe, which I call Honey Barbecue Sauce. Grilling the pork tenderloin using the indirect method keeps it moist and juicy. Serve with Grilled Corn in the Husk and watermelon wedges.

Honey Barbecue Sauce

1 cup ketchup

½ cup honey

2 tablespoons cider vinegar

1 tablespoon Dijon mustard

2 teaspoons Worcestershire sauce

1 teaspoon steak sauce

¼ teaspoon hot pepper sauce

1 pork tenderloin (1½ pounds)

294 Calories
34.0 g Protein
25.9 g Carbohydrates
5.9 g Fat
18.1% Calories from Fat
0.5 g Fiber
510 mg Sodium
107 mg Cholesterol

To make Honey Barbecue Sauce

Combine ketchup, honey, cider vinegar, mustard, Worcestershire sauce, steak sauce, and hot pepper sauce in a medium saucepan over moderately low heat and cook 30 minutes, stirring occasionally. Store honey barbecue sauce in a covered container in the refrigerator. Makes $1\frac{1}{4}$ cups.

WHEN READY TO GRILL

Place a drip pan in the center of the lower grate and place an equal number of briquettes on both sides. When coals are hot, place the pork over the coals and sear it for 1 minute on each side. Move the pork directly over the drip pan and brush with Honey Barbecue Sauce. Cover grill and cook 20 to 25 minutes, or until a meat thermometer registers 150 to 155°, turning pork every 15 minutes and brushing with barbecue sauce each time. Allow pork to sit for 5 minutes before carving it into thin slices.

4 SERVINGS

This is a fabulous entree because it is both easy to prepare and exceptionally flavorful. Serve with grilled Zucchini and Yellow Squash Ribbons and roasted new potatoes.

Marinade

5 tablespoons red wine vinegar
½ tablespoon extra-virgin olive oil
1 teaspoon *each* oregano and thyme

1 boneless loin pork roast (1¼ pounds), all visible fat removed

Mustard Sauce

¼ cup egg substitute
2 tablespoons *each* fresh lemon juice and Dijon mustard
1 tablespoon honey
1 clove garlic, minced

Parsley

342 Calories
35.9 g Protein
6.8 g Carbohydrates
18.3 g Fat
48.2% Calories from Fat
0.1 g Fiber
304 mg Sodium
91 mg Cholesterol

To make marinade

Combine vinegar, olive oil, oregano, and thyme in a non-metal dish (or a 1-gallon reclosable plastic bag). Add pork roast and turn to coat both sides. Cover dish and refrigerate several hours or overnight, turning pork at least once.

WHEN READY TO GRILL

Over hot coals, place pork roast on a grill coated with non-stick vegetable spray. Sear the pork for 1 minute on each side. Cover grill and cook 12 to 14 minutes or until a meat thermometer registers 150 to 155°, turning pork every 5 minutes. Allow pork roast to sit for 5 minutes before carving it into thin slices.

To make Mustard Sauce

While pork is cooking, combine egg substitute, lemon juice, mustard, honey, and garlic in a small heavy saucepan over moderate heat. Cook, stirring frequently, until sauce is warm. Set aside and keep warm.

WHEN READY TO SERVE

Divide pork among four dinner plates. Spoon 2 tablespoons Mustard Sauce over each serving and garnish with fresh parsley.

4 SERVINGS

This orange marmalade marinade not only glazes the pork roast
as it cooks but imbues it with a deliciously rich flavor and keeps it moist
and juicy. Serve with Grilled Yams and a mixed green salad.

Marinade
¼ cup orange marmalade
2 tablespoons *each* Dijon mustard and reduced-fat
  creamy peanut butter
1 tablespoon fresh lemon juice
½ tablespoon extra-virgin olive oil
1 teaspoon white horseradish
⅛ teaspoon *each* salt and freshly ground pepper

1 boneless loin pork roast (1½ pounds)

To make marinade
Combine orange marmalade, Dijon mustard, peanut
butter, lemon juice, olive oil, horseradish, salt, and pepper in a nonmetal dish (or a 1-gallon reclosable plastic
bag). Add pork roast and turn to coat both sides. Cover
dish and refrigerate several hours or overnight, turning pork at least once.

425 Calories
36.8 g Protein
16.2 g Carbohydrates
22.2 g Fat
47.1% Calories from Fat
0.4 g Fiber
401 mg Sodium
91 mg Cholesterol

WHEN READY TO GRILL
Over hot coals, place pork roast (reserve marinade) on a
grill coated with nonstick vegetable spray. Sear the pork
roast for 1 minute on each side. Cover grill and cook 18 to
22 minutes or until a meat thermometer registers 150 to
155°, turning pork every 5 minutes and brushing with reserved marinade after pork has cooked for 12 minutes.
Allow pork roast to sit for 5 minutes before carving it into
thin slices.

4 SERVINGS

*The intensity of the fresh dill in the sauce highlights the flavor
of the pork. I like to marinate the pork chops in half the sauce and
save the remainder to spoon over them once they are cooked. The leftover
pork can also be thinly sliced and stuffed into a whole wheat pita
pocket with thinly sliced tomatoes and sweet onions topped with alfalfa sprouts
for a great snack or lunch. Serve with Couscous and Vegetable Salad (page 88).*

Dill Sauce

6 tablespoons *each* Grey Poupon peppercorn
   mustard and fresh lemon juice
¼ cup lowfat plain yogurt
3 tablespoons chopped fresh dill
½ teaspoon freshly ground pepper

4 butterfly pork chops (6 ounces each), cut
   1 inch thick

To make Dill Sauce

Combine mustard, lemon juice, yogurt, dill, and pepper in a nonmetal dish. Remove ½ cup Dill Sauce and refrigerate, covered, until ready to serve. Add pork chops to dish and turn to coat both sides. Cover dish and refrigerate several hours or overnight.

WHEN READY TO GRILL

Over hot coals, place pork chops on a grill coated with nonstick vegetable spray. Sear the pork chops for 1 minute on each side. Cover grill and cook 6 to 8 minutes on each side or until a meat thermometer registers 155°.

WHEN READY TO SERVE

Divide chops among four dinner plates and spoon 2 tablespoons of the reserved dill sauce over each one. Garnish each serving with a sprig of fresh dill, if desired.

329 Calories
43.2 g Protein
2.5 g Carbohydrates
15.2 g Fat
41.7% Calories from Fat
0.0 g Fiber
408 mg Sodium
129 mg Cholesterol

6 SERVINGS

Serve this versatile, savory pork tenderloin with rice pilaf and a cucumber salad. Leftovers are delicious when slices of cold pork are stuffed into pita bread and topped with a Greek salad, or when cubes of pork are added to homemade black bean or pea soup.

Marinade
¼ cup soy sauce

2 tablespoons light rum

2 tablespoons firmly packed dark brown sugar

½ teaspoon ground ginger

¼ teaspoon *each* mustard, paprika, and freshly ground pepper

⅛ teaspoon each cayenne and salt

1 pork tenderloin (2 pounds)

Caramelized Onions
1 medium Bermuda onion, thinly sliced

1 can (6 ounces) pineapple juice

227 Calories
30.5 g Protein
12.6 g Carbohydrates
5.0 g Fat
20.0% Calories from Fat
0.5 g Fiber
804 mg Sodium
95 mg Cholesterol

To make marinade

Combine soy sauce, rum, brown sugar, ginger, mustard, paprika, pepper, cayenne, and salt in a nonmetal dish (or a 1-gallon reclosable plastic bag). Add pork tenderloin and turn to coat both sides. Cover dish and refrigerate several hours or overnight, turning pork at least once.

Before cooking tenderloin, soak 1 cup smoking wood chips according to package instructions while the coals are getting hot.

To make Caramelized Onions

While coals are getting hot, combine the onion slices and pineapple juice in a medium saucepan over moderate heat. Bring to a boil and cook over moderately high heat for 30 minutes, or until all the liquid has evaporated. Keep warm.

WHEN READY TO GRILL

When coals are hot, sprinkle wet chips over them. Place pork tenderloin (reserve marinade) over hot coals on a grill coated with nonstick vegetable spray. Sear the pork for 1 minute on each side. Cover grill and cook 15 to 18 minutes, or until a meat thermometer registers 150 to 155°, turning pork every 5 minutes and brushing with reserved marinade the last 6 minutes of cooking time. Allow pork to sit for 5 minutes before carving it into thin slices.

WHEN READY TO SERVE

Divide sliced pork among four dinner plates, spooning onions over each serving.

4 SERVINGS

*Tangerines and apricots team up to make a marvelous marinade and sauce in
this pork entree. Serve with a combination of risotto and peas and a spinach salad.*

Marinade
½ cup fresh tangerine juice

2 tablespoons Madeira

1 tablespoon apricot preserves

1 tablespoon *each* white wine vinegar and honey

½ tablespoon extra-virgin olive oil

1 teaspoon rosemary

½ teaspoon freshly ground white pepper

2 cloves garlic, minced

1 pork tenderloin (1½ pounds)

Tangerine Sauce
¾ cup tangerine juice

1½ tablespoons cornstarch

4 dried apricots, slivered

2 tablespoons honey mustard

1 teaspoon rice vinegar

⅛ teaspoon *each* salt and freshly ground
  white pepper

1 tangerine, peeled and cut into segments

300 Calories
34.2 g Protein
23.9 g Carbohydrates
6.9 g Fat
20.6% Calories from Fat
1.0 g Fiber
147 mg Sodium
107 mg Cholesterol

To make marinade

Combine tangerine juice, Madeira, apricot preserves, white wine vinegar, honey, olive oil, rosemary, pepper, and garlic in a small saucepan over moderate heat. Cook 4 minutes. Place pork tenderloin in a nonmetal dish (or a 1-gallon reclosable plastic bag) and pour warm marinade over top. Turn to coat both sides. Cover dish and refrigerate several hours or overnight, turning pork at least once.

WHEN READY TO GRILL

Over hot coals, place pork tenderloin (reserve marinade) on a grill coated with nonstick vegetable spray. Sear the pork for 1 minute on each side. Cover grill and cook 15 to 18 minutes or until a meat thermometer registers 150 to 155°, turning pork every 5 minutes and basting with reserved marinade the last 6 minutes of cooking time.

To make Tangerine Sauce

While pork tenderloin is cooking, combine tangerine juice and cornstarch in a small heavy saucepan and blend well. Add apricots, honey mustard, rice vinegar, salt, and pepper and blend well. Place saucepan over moderate heat and cook 6 to 7 minutes or until sauce thickens, stirring occasionally. Add tangerine segments and keep warm.

WHEN READY TO SERVE

Carve pork tenderloin into thin slices. Divide it among four dinner plates, spooning sauce over each serving.

6 SERVINGS

The currant jelly in the marinade gives a sweetness to the pork that is balanced by the tangy applesauce. If you do not want to make the applesauce from scratch, just add some prepared horseradish to your favorite store-bought applesauce.

Marinade

1 clove garlic

¼ cup tamari

¼ cup currant jelly

2 tablespoons medium dry sherry

½ teaspoon *each* dry mustard and thyme

1 piece fresh ginger root, peeled and cut
   ¼ inch thick

1 pork tenderloin (2 pounds)

Tangy Applesauce

1½ pounds MacIntosh apples, peeled, cored,
   and quartered

¼ cup sugar

¼ cup water

1 (3-inch) vanilla bean, split into 2 pieces

1 (3-inch) cinnamon stick

2 tablespoons white horseradish

297 Calories
30.9 g Protein
31.4 g Carbohydrates
5.3 g Fat
15.9% Calories from Fat
1.8 g Fiber
750 mg Sodium
95 mg Cholesterol

To make marinade

In work bowl of food processor fitted with a metal blade, process garlic until chopped. Add tamari, currant jelly, sherry, mustard, and thyme and blend well. Add ginger root but do not process.

Place pork in a nonmetal dish (or a 1-gallon reclosable plastic bag) and pour marinade over top. Turn to coat both sides. Cover dish and refrigerate several hours or overnight, turning pork at least once.

To make Tangy Applesauce

In clean work bowl of food processor, process apples until finely chopped. Transfer apples to a medium saucepan over moderately low heat and add sugar, water, vanilla bean, and cinnamon stick. Cover saucepan and cook 25 minutes, stirring occasionally. Bring applesauce to room temperature. Remove cinnamon stick and add horseradish; blend well. Refrigerate, covered, until ready to serve.

WHEN READY TO GRILL

Over hot coals, place the pork tenderloin (reserve marinade) on a grill coated with nonstick vegetable spray. Sear the pork for 1 minute on each side. Cover grill and cook 15 to 18 minutes, or until a meat thermometer registers 150 to 155°, turning pork every 5 minutes and brushing with reserved marinade the last 6 minutes of cooking time. Allow pork to sit for 5 minutes before carving into thin slices.

WHEN READY TO SERVE

Divide the pork tenderloin slices among six dinner plates and accompany each serving with Tangy Applesauce.

6 SERVINGS

*Slices of pork with prune and apple filling covered with
red currant sauce are spectacular to look at and wonderful to eat.
Serve with a sweet potato and carrot puree and grilled Apple Rings.*

6 to 8 bite-size prunes
3 tablespoons Madeira

1 pork boneless loin roast (2 pounds), all visible
    fat removed
1 small apple, cubed
½ teaspoon salt
¼ teaspoon freshly ground pepper
2 tablespoons Madeira

Currant Sauce
¾ cup currant jelly
1 tablespoon dry mustard
1 tablespoon Madeira

402 Calories
30.8 g Protein
34.0 g Carbohydrates
15.1 g Fat
33.7% Calories from Fat
1.0 g Fiber
262 mg Sodium
81 mg Cholesterol

Place prunes in a small nonmetal dish and cover with 3 tablespoons Madeira. Cover dish and allow it to sit for several hours or overnight.

Using a sharp knife, make a hole in the center of each end of the pork roast. Push the handle of a wooden spoon through entire length of roast, turning to make a tunnel approximately ½ inch in diameter. Alternately stuff prunes (reserve Madeira) and apple cubes into tunnel, pushing from both ends. Sew openings shut at both ends with poultry lacer or large needle and heavy thread. Place roast in a nonmetal dish and sprinkle with salt and pepper. Pour 2 more tablespoons Madeira along with the reserved Madeira over roast. Cover dish and refrigerate several hours.

WHEN READY TO GRILL
Prepare a grill with a drip pan in the center of the lower grate and place an equal number of briquettes on both sides of the pan. When coals are hot, place the pork roast (reserve the marinade) over the coals on a grill coated with nonstick vegetable spray. Sear the pork for 1 minute on each side. Move the pork directly over the drip pan. Cover grill and cook 1 hour and 15 minutes, or until a meat thermometer registers150 to 155°, brushing occasionally with reserved marinade.

To make Currant Sauce
While the pork is cooking, combine jelly, mustard, and Madeira in a small heavy saucepan over moderately low heat. Bring to a boil, stirring occasionally. Continue cooking until sauce is smooth. Keep warm.

WHEN READY TO SERVE
Carve roast into thin slices and divide it among six dinner plates. Spoon about 2 tablespoons of Currant Sauce over each serving.

4 SERVINGS

This recipe was featured in a Des Moines Register *article on grilling. It was contributed by the National Pork Producers, culinary experts when it comes to preparing a succulent pork dish. Serve with Grilled Acorn Squash stuffed with brown rice.*

1 pork tenderloin (1 pound), cut into
    ¾-inch cubes
⅓ cup smoky barbecue sauce
⅓ cup orange marmalade
2 tablespoons horseradish

WHEN READY TO GRILL
Thread tenderloin cubes onto skewers (if using bamboo skewers, soak in water 30 minutes before using to prevent burning). Stir together remaining ingredients for basting sauce. Over medium-hot coals, place kebabs, brushing generously with basting sauce, on a grill. Grill and turn to brown evenly, brushing frequently with sauce until just done, 10 to 12 minutes.

177 Calories
22.1 g Protein
11.1 g Carbohydrates
3.9 g Fat
19.7% Calories from Fat
0.1 g Fiber
217 mg Sodium
71 mg Cholesterol

4 SERVINGS

The name yard beans *is appropriate because the beans can actually grow to be a full yard in length. Yard beans are available at most Asian food stores. Serve with steamed brown basmati rice.*

Marinade

2 tablespoons soy sauce

1 tablespoon rice wine

1 teaspoon *each* honey and red wine vinegar

1 teaspoon hot bean paste

1 pork tenderloin (12 ounces), thinly sliced

1 pound yard beans, cut into 2-inch lengths

1 red pepper, cut into ⅛-inch slices

4 green onions, cut into 2-inch lengths

To make marinade

Combine soy sauce, rice wine, honey, vinegar, and hot bean paste in a nonmetal dish. Add pork and toss to coat pieces. Cover dish and refrigerate several hours.

Place beans in a large pot of boiling water and cook 3 minutes, or until beans are tender but still crisp. Drain and set aside in a covered dish.

WHEN READY TO GRILL

Over hot coals, place a grilling wok coated with nonstick vegetable spray on a grill. Add pork (reserve marinade) and stir-fry for 1 minute. Cover grill and cook 3 minutes. Repeat process. Add beans, pepper, and green onions; stir-fry 1 minute. Cover grill and cook 2 minutes. Repeat process one more time. Remove stir-fry to serving dish; pour reserved marinade over top and blend well.

170 Calories
20.3 g Protein
14.8 g Carbohydrates
3.0 g Fat
15.8% Calories from Fat
2.5 g Fiber
560 mg Sodium
54 mg Cholesterol

4 SERVINGS

*This sensational pork roast is exceptionally moist and flavorful.
The marinade imbues a fabulous flavor throughout the pork, and it
would also enhance the flavor of a leg of lamb or pork chops.
Serve with Mediterranean Rice Pilaf (page 116) and Grilled Bananas.*

Marinade
¼ cup tamari
2 tablespoons dry sherry
1 tablespoon honey
½ tablespoon dry mustard
1 piece fresh ginger root, peeled and cut
    ¼ inch thick

1 boneless loin pork roast (1½ pounds)

To make marinade
Combine tamari, sherry, honey, mustard, and ginger
root in a nonmetal dish (or a 1-gallon reclosable plastic
bag). Add pork roast and turn to coat both sides. Cover
dish and refrigerate several hours or overnight, turning pork at least once.

WHEN READY TO GRILL
Over hot coals, place pork (reserve marinade) on a grill
coated with nonstick vegetable spray. Cover grill and cook
35 to 45 minutes, or until a meat thermometer registers
150 to 155°, turning pork every 5 minutes and basting with
marinade the last 15 minutes of cooking time. Allow pork
to sit for 5 minutes before carving into thin slices.

328 Calories
36.1 g Protein
5.5 g Carbohydrates
16.7 g Fat
45.8% Calories from Fat
0.0 g Fiber
1088 mg Sodium
91 mg Cholesterol

4 SERVINGS

These delectable pork chops are the best! The marinade infuses the pork with a fabulous flavor and tenderizes it as well. Serve with grilled Vegetable Salad.

Marinade

½ cup fresh tangerine juice
2 tablespoons tamari
1 tablespoon honey
1 teaspoon *each* extra-virgin olive oil and
   rice vinegar
⅛ teaspoon freshly ground pepper

4 top loin pork chops (6 ounces each), cut
   ¾ inch thick

To make marinade

Combine tangerine juice, tamari, honey, olive oil, rice vinegar, and pepper in a nonmetal dish. Add pork chops and turn to coat both sides. Cover dish and refrigerate several hours or overnight, turning pork at least once.

WHEN READY TO GRILL

Over hot coals, place pork chops on a grill coated with nonstick vegetable spray. Sear the pork chops for 1 minute on each side. Cover grill and cook 4 to 5 minutes on each side or until a meat thermometer registers 150 to 155°.

271 Calories
35.1 g Protein
4.0 g Carbohydrates
11.9 g Fat
39.4% Calories from Fat
0.0 g Fiber
336 mg Sodium
107 mg Cholesterol

4 SERVINGS

The teriyaki marinade harmonizes with the pork, pineapple, and vegetables to create a sensational kebab. Serve with grilled Pineapple Rings and steamed basmati rice.

Marinade

¼ cup tamari

2 tablespoons *each* honey and sherry

½ teaspoon sesame oil

1 clove garlic, minced

1 piece fresh ginger root, peeled and cut
   ¼ inch thick

1 boneless loin pork roast (1¼ pounds), cut into
   1½-inch cubes

Kebab Fruit and Vegetables

8 (1-inch) cubes pineapple

8 shiitake mushrooms, stemmed

4 green onions, each cut into two 2-inch lengths

8 (1-inch) cubes red pepper

346 Calories
31.3 g Protein
20.7 g Carbohydrates
14.5 g Fat
37.7% Calories from Fat
1.4 g Fiber
1079 mg Sodium
76 mg Cholesterol

To make marinade

Combine tamari, honey, sherry, sesame oil, garlic, and ginger root in a nonmetal dish (or a 1-gallon reclosable plastic bag). Add pork and toss to coat all over. Cover dish and refrigerate several hours or overnight, turning pork cubes at least once.

WHEN READY TO GRILL

Alternate pieces of pork (reserve marinade and discard ginger root), pineapple, mushrooms, green onions, and red pepper on metal skewers. Over hot coals, place skewers on a grill coated with nonstick vegetable spray. Cover grill and cook 8 to 9 minutes, turning kebabs every 3 minutes and brushing with the marinade the last 6 minutes of cooking time.

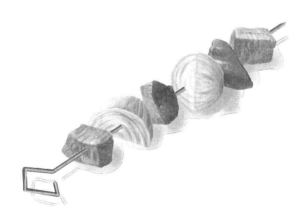

4 SERVINGS

*The delicious combination of ham, fruit, and vegetables
glazed with teriyaki sauce is a quick and easy way to please
your family. Serve with steamed rice and grilled Pineapple Rings.*

Teriyaki Sauce
¼ cup hoisin sauce
3 tablespoons pineapple juice
1 tablespoon Worcestershire sauce

1 extra-lean turkey ham (1 pound), cut into
  1½-inch cubes

Kebab Fruit and Vegetables
1 medium pineapple, cubed
1 Bermuda onion, cut into 8 wedges
1 green pepper, cut into 8 cubes
8 mushrooms

To make Teriyaki Sauce
Combine hoisin sauce, pineapple juice, and Worcestershire sauce in a small bowl and blend well.

WHEN READY TO GRILL
Alternate ham, pineapple, onion, pepper, and mushrooms
onto 8 skewers. Over hot coals, place skewers on a grill
coated with nonstick vegetable spray. Brush ham, pineapple, and vegetables with some of the sauce. Cover grill and
cook 8 to 9 minutes, turning skewers every 3 minutes and
brushing with sauce.

271 Calories
24.7 g Protein
27.8 g Carbohydrates
7.1 g Fat
36.6% Calories from Fat
3.2 g Fiber
1567 mg Sodium
144 mg Cholesterol

4 SERVINGS

The contrast of sweet and peppery ingredients in the marinade endows the pork with a marvelous flavor. Serve with Grilled Acorn Squash and Mediterranean Rice Pilaf (page 116).

Marinade

¼ cup soy sauce

2 tablespoons *each* bourbon and honey

1 teaspoon ground ginger

⅛ teaspoon freshly ground white pepper

⅛ teaspoon hot pepper sauce

2 cloves garlic, minced

1 pork tenderloin (1½ pounds)

To make marinade

Combine soy sauce, bourbon, honey, ginger, white pepper, hot pepper sauce, and garlic in a nonmetal dish (or a 1-gallon reclosable plastic bag). Add pork tenderloin and turn to coat both sides. Cover dish and refrigerate several hours or overnight, turning pork at least once.

WHEN READY TO GRILL

Over hot coals, place pork (reserve marinade) on a grill coated with nonstick vegetable spray. Sear pork for 1 minute on each side. Cover grill and cook 15 to 18 minutes, or until a meat thermometer registers 150 to 155°, turning pork every 5 minutes and brushing with reserved marinade the last 6 minutes of cooking time. Allow pork to sit for 5 minutes before carving into thin slices.

244 Calories
34.4 g Protein
10.9 g Carbohydrates
5.6 g Fat
20.7% Calories from Fat
0.1 g Fiber
1109 mg Sodium
107 mg Cholesterol

SEAFOOD

4 SERVINGS

The boldness of the Cajun-spiced red snapper is tempered by the Lemon Butter Sauce. It is an excellent entree to serve with lemon rice pilaf and Grilled Asparagus.

2 teaspoons Cajun Magic Blackened Redfish Seasoning
2 Red Snapper filets (12 ounces each), halved

Lemon Butter Sauce
2 tablespoons fresh lemon juice
¼ cup light margarine
1 tablespoon minced parsley

WHEN READY TO GRILL
Sprinkle ½ teaspoon seasoning on each side of a red snapper filet. Over hot coals, place filets on a grill coated with nonstick vegetable spray. Cover grill and cook 4 minutes on each side.

To make Lemon Butter Sauce
While fish is cooking, bring lemon juice to a boil in a small saucepan over moderate heat. Remove pan from heat and add margarine; blend well. Add parsley just before serving.

WHEN READY TO SERVE
Spoon 1½ tablespoons Lemon Butter Sauce over each blackened fish. Garnish with a sprig of parsley, if desired.

215 Calories
33.6 g Protein
0.7 g Carbohydrates
7.9 g Fat
33.0% Calories from Fat
0.0 g Fiber
440 mg Sodium
60 mg Cholesterol

4 SERVINGS

Ginger Oil and Ginger Sauce combine to subtly enhance the flavor of shark.
Serve with lemon rice pilaf and a blend of steamed carrots and zucchini.

Ginger Oil

½ cup extra-virgin olive oil

1 piece fresh ginger root, peeled and cut
¼ inch thick

Ginger Sauce

¼ cup sugar

1 can (14½ ounces) fatfree chicken broth

2 tablespoons chopped fresh ginger root

4 blackfin shark filets (5 ounces each)*

4 teaspoons ginger oil

*If shark is unavailable, substitute swordfish, marlin, or tuna.

196 Calories
21.3 g Protein
7.0 g Carbohydrates
8.8 g Fat
40.5% Calories from Fat
0.0 g Fiber
304 mg Sodium
50 mg Cholesterol

To make Ginger Oil

Combine oil and ginger root in a small heavy saucepan over moderate heat and bring to a boil. Remove saucepan from heat, cover, and let sit for 30 minutes. Pour Ginger Oil into a glass jar with a tight fitting lid and store in a dark, cool place. Use as needed. Makes $\frac{1}{2}$ cup.

To make Ginger Sauce

Pour sugar into a small heavy saucepan over moderate heat for 5 to 6 minutes, or until the sugar begins to melt. Swirl the pan over the heat to melt sugar evenly. Add chicken broth and ginger and cook over high heat for 8 to 10 minutes, or until the mixture is reduced to 1 cup. Keep Ginger Sauce warm until ready to serve.

WHEN READY TO GRILL
Brush each shark filet with $\frac{1}{2}$ teaspoon Ginger Oil. Over hot coals, place shark filet, oiled side down, on a grill coated with nonstick vegetable spray. Brush top of each filet with $\frac{1}{2}$ teaspoon Ginger Oil, cover grill, and cook 5 minutes on each side.

WHEN READY TO SERVE
Spoon about 2 tablespoons Ginger Sauce over each shark filet. Garnish each serving with a piece of slivered lemon peel.

4 SERVINGS

Marlin's strong flavor is greatly enhanced by cooking it on a grill. The unusual Tangerine Sauce will also complement other kinds of fish. Serve with orange-glazed carrots and a fresh fruit salad.

WHEN READY TO SERVE
Spoon a heaping tablespoon Tangerine Sauce over each filet and garnish with tangerine wedges on the side.

4 Blue Marlin filets (6 ounces each)*
4 teaspoons Ginger Oil (page 186)

Tangerine Sauce

2 tablespoons light margarine
¼ cup (2 ounces) finely chopped shallots
1 tablespoon white wine vinegar
¼ cup fresh tangerine juice
1 teaspoon Dijon mustard

WHEN READY TO GRILL
Brush one side of each blue marlin filet with ½ teaspoon Ginger Oil. Over hot coals, place filets, oiled side down, on a grill coated with nonstick vegetable spray. Brush top of each filet with ½ teaspoon ginger oil, cover grill, and cook 5 minutes on each side.

To make Tangerine Sauce

While fish is cooking, melt margarine in a small heavy saucepan over moderate heat. Add shallots and cook 3 minutes. Add white wine vinegar and cook 1 minute. Add tangerine juice and cook 3 minutes, stirring frequently. Add mustard and blend well.

*If marlin is unavailable, substitute tuna or salmon.

291 Calories
35.3 g Protein
3.1 g Carbohydrates
14.7 g Fat
45.4% Calories from Fat
0.1 g Fiber
160 mg Sodium
57 mg Cholesterol

4 SERVINGS

This recipe was given to me by a neighbor who is a fabulous cook and hostess. The marinade has a nice balance of lemon, soy sauce, and Dijon mustard that marries well with tuna. Serve with grilled Greek Vegetables.

Marinade

⅓ cup soy sauce

¼ cup fresh lemon juice

2 tablespoons extra-virgin olive oil

2 teaspoons Dijon mustard

1 heaping teaspoon finely grated lemon peel

1 large clove garlic, minced

4 tuna steaks (6 ounces each)*

2 star fruit, cut into ¼-inch slices

To make marinade

Combine soy sauce, lemon juice, olive oil, mustard, lemon peel, and garlic in a nonmetal dish. Add tuna and turn to coat both sides. Cover dish and refrigerate for 30 minutes.

WHEN READY TO GRILL

Over hot coals, place tuna steaks on a grill coated with nonstick vegetable spray. Cover grill and cook 5 minutes on each side.

*If fresh tuna is unavailable, substitute shark, salmon, or swordfish.

WHEN READY TO SERVE

Garnish tuna with star fruit slices as soon as they are removed from grill.

284 Calories
37.2 g Protein
6.9 g Carbohydrates
11.3 g Fat
35.9% Calories from Fat
0.6 g Fiber
784 mg Sodium
60 mg Cholesterol

4 SERVINGS

*Most people are surprised at how good sea bass is. It tastes
almost like lobster. The touch of Ginger Oil is all that is needed to bring
out its wonderful flavor. Serve with rice pilaf and grilled Pineapple Rings.*

4 sea bass filets (5 ounces each)
4 teaspoon Ginger Oil (page 186)

WHEN READY TO GRILL
Brush one side of each sea bass filet with ½ teaspoon
Ginger Oil. Over hot coals, place filet, oiled side down, on
a grill coated with nonstick vegetable spray. Brush top of
each filet with ½ teaspoon Ginger Oil, cover grill, and cook
5 to 6 minutes on each side.

182 Calories
27.5 g Protein
0.0 g Carbohydrates
7.3 g Fat
36.1% Calories from Fat
0.0 g Fiber
101 mg Sodium
62 mg Cholesterol

4 SERVINGS

This versatile recipe combines many of the same ingredients used to make a Greek salad. It can be enjoyed immediately after it has been grilled, served the next day as a cold salmon salad, or spooned into whole wheat pita bread.

Dressing

1 clove garlic

3 tablespoons fresh lemon juice

1 tablespoon extra-virgin olive oil

¾ teaspoon *each* oregano and dry mustard

¼ teaspoon *each* salt and freshly ground pepper

1 salmon filet (1½ pounds), cut into 4 pieces and skin removed

¼ cup *each* chopped roma tomatoes, green pepper, Bermuda onion, cilantro, and parsley

4 ounces feta cheese, crumbled

To make dressing

In work bowl of food processor fitted with metal blade, chop garlic. Add lemon juice, olive oil, oregano, mustard, salt, and pepper and process until smooth.

Cut four pieces of aluminum foil large enough to enclose each piece of salmon. Place a piece of salmon on foil and top each one with a tablespoonful of tomatoes, green pepper, onion, cilantro, parsley, and 2 tablespoons of feta. Pour 2 teaspoons dressing over each salmon and close foil to securely seal the fish and vegetables.

WHEN READY TO GRILL

Over hot coals, place packets of fish on a grill. Cover grill and cook 12 minutes or until salmon is no longer pink. To test for doneness, open aluminum foil and insert a knife into center of salmon. If additional cooking time is necessary, rewrap the salmon in foil.

344 Calories

37.2 g Protein

4.3 g Carbohydrates

19.0 g Fat

49.6% Calories from Fat

0.6 g Fiber

527 mg Sodium

116 mg Cholesterol

4 SERVINGS

I use frozen lobster tail in this recipe because I have trouble dropping a live one into a pot of boiling water. (Of course, fresh lobster can be used as well.) Either way, grilled lobster combined with the Sesame Seed Dressing and condiments is fabulous!

WHEN READY TO SERVE

Place 1½ cups mixed greens on each dinner plate. Divide lobster among mixed greens and top with 2 tablespoons carrots, 2 tablespoons beets, and papaya. Drizzle 3 to 4 tablespoons dressing over each salad.

Sesame Seed Dressing

1 small garlic clove
1 tablespoon *each* tamari and sherry vinegar
½ teaspoon Dijon mustard
½ teaspoon sesame oil
½ cup canola oil

1 frozen lobster (1¼ pounds), thawed
  and cleaned
2 teaspoons extra-virgin olive oil

6 cups mixed greens
½ cup *each* julienned carrots and beets
1 large papaya, peeled and diced

To make dressing

In work bowl of food processor fitted with a metal blade, process garlic until chopped. Add tamari, sherry vinegar, mustard, and sesame oil and blend well. Add canola oil in a slow steady stream until well blended. Set aside.

WHEN READY TO GRILL

Brush each side of lobster with 1 teaspoon olive oil. Over hot coals, place lobster on a grill coated with nonstick vegetable spray. Cover grill and cook 12 to 14 minutes or until lobster is no longer translucent, turning lobster every 4 minutes. Remove shell and cut lobster into bite-size pieces.

385 Calories
19.5 g Protein
12.0 g Carbohydrates
29.5 g Fat
68.9% Calories from Fat
2.0 g Fiber
612 mg Sodium
59 mg Cholesterol

4 SERVINGS

*This marinade is a quick and easy way to bring out the true flavors
of marlin. It will also enhance the flavors of swordfish or sea bass.
Serve with Grilled Ratatouille and steamed basmati rice.*

Marinade

6 tablespoons fresh lemon juice

2 tablespoons extra-virgin olive oil

2 tablespoons *each* finely chopped parsley and
    green onion

1½ teaspoons *each* thyme and oregano

2 cloves garlic, minced

2 marlin filets (12 ounces each)

To make marinade

Combine lemon juice, olive oil, parsley, green onion,
thyme, oregano, and garlic in a nonmetal dish. Add marlin and turn to coat both sides. Cover dish and refrigerate for 30 minutes.

WHEN READY TO GRILL

Over hot coals, place marlin on a grill coated with nonstick
vegetable spray. Cover grill and cook 5 minutes on
each side.

WHEN READY TO SERVE

Cut each marlin filet
into 2 pieces. Garnish
each serving with
lemon wedges and a
sprig of parsley.

267 Calories
37.6 g Protein
2.3 g Carbohydrates
11.3 g Fat
38.0% Calories from Fat
0.2 g Fiber
64 mg Sodium
61 mg Cholesterol

4 SERVINGS

*On a recent trip to Seattle, I had this delicious salad
at a seafood restaurant. I have adapted it to be lower in fat,
and it is still delicious and satisfying. Serve with sourdough bread.*

Croutons

3 slices nonfat bread, cubed
2 tablespoons extra-virgin olive oil
2 cloves garlic, halved
⅛ teaspoon *each* salt, thyme, and freshly
    ground pepper

Dressing

2 large cloves garlic
¼ cup fresh lemon juice
3 tablespoons extra-virgin olive oil
2 tablespoons water
1 tablespoon Dijon mustard
1 teaspoon anchovy paste
¾ teaspoon Worcestershire sauce
⅛ teaspoon *each* turmeric and freshly
    ground pepper

448 Calories
28.3 g Protein
18.5 g Carbohydrates
28.7 g Fat
57.7% Calories from Fat
2.0 g Fiber
724 mg Sodium
66 mg Cholesterol

1 salmon filet (1 pound)
½ tablespoon extra-virgin olive oil
¼ teaspoon freshly ground lemon pepper

½ pound fresh spinach, washed, stemmed, and
    torn into bite-size pieces
¼ cup shredded fresh parmesan cheese

To make croutons

Preheat oven to 350°.

Place bread cubes on a baking sheet and bake for 12 to 14 minutes, or until golden brown.

Place 2 tablespoons olive oil and halved garlic cloves in a large frying pan over moderately low heat. Add bread cubes, salt, thyme, and pepper and cook 1 to 2 minutes, stirring frequently. Set aside in a covered container.

To make dressing

In work bowl of food processor fitted with a metal blade, process garlic until finely chopped. Add lemon juice, 3 tablespoons olive oil, water, mustard, anchovy paste, Worcestershire sauce, turmeric, and pepper and process until smooth. Set aside.

WHEN READY TO GRILL

Brush both sides of salmon with $\frac{1}{2}$ tablespoon olive oil and sprinkle with lemon pepper. Place salmon, skin side up, on a grill coated with nonstick vegetable spray. Cover grill and cook 1 minute. Turn salmon over, cover grill, and cook 10 minutes or until salmon is no longer pink inside. Allow to cool to room temperature. Remove skin and cut salmon into small pieces.

WHEN READY TO SERVE

Place spinach in a large salad bowl. Pour dressing over top and toss well. Add salmon, croutons, and parmesan cheese and blend well. Divide the salmon salad among four dinner plates.

4 SERVINGS

*Tomatillos are a Mexican green tomato that resemble cherry tomatoes,
but are firmer, more tart, and a spicier addition to fiery dishes, such as salsas.
Combining the tomatillo salsa with the traditional fajita ingredients—grilled tuna,
onions, and green pepper—adds a new dimension to this popular Mexican dish.
Serve with Mexican Corn Soup and a fresh fruit salad.*

Sonia's Tomatillo Salsa

3 tomatillos
½ tablespoon extra-virgin olive oil
½ cup packed chopped cilantro
2 jalapeños, seeded*
1 clove garlic
¼ teaspoon salt
3 tablespoons fresh lime juice
½ cup plain nonfat yogurt

Marinade

¼ cup fresh lemon juice
½ tablespoon extra-virgin olive oil
¼ cup packed, chopped cilantro
1 clove garlic, chopped
⅛ teaspoon freshly ground pepper

1 yellowfin tuna filet (9 ounces)

½ tablespoon extra-virgin olive oil
1 medium Bermuda onion, thinly sliced
1 medium green pepper, thinly sliced
4 (7-inch) fajita shells
2 roma tomatoes, diced

*The seeds of jalapeño peppers are very hot. To avoid burning your skin, wear rubber or latex gloves when removing the seeds. Immediately wash knife, cutting surface, and gloves.

To make Sonia's Tomatillo Salsa

Peel off husks and stems and wash to remove the sticky resinous material covering the tomatillos. Thinly slice the tomatillos.

In small frying pan over medium-high heat, heat olive oil. Add tomatillos and cook 4 minutes, stirring frequently. Set aside.

In work bowl of food processor fitted with metal blade, process ½ cup cilantro, jalapeños, and garlic. Add tomatillos and process until blended. Add salt, lime juice, and yogurt and process until just blended. Transfer salsa to a covered container and refrigerate for up to 4 hours.

To make marinade

Combine lemon juice, olive oil, cilantro, garlic, and pepper in a nonmetal dish. Add tuna and turn to coat both sides. Cover dish and refrigerate for 30 minutes.

WHEN READY TO GRILL

Pour olive oil into a plastic bag and add sliced onions and green pepper; turn to coat all over. Over hot coals, place onions and green pepper in a grilling wok coated with nonstick vegetable spray. Cover grill and cook 12 to 16 minutes, or until vegetables are golden brown and tender, turning every 4 minutes. Set aside.

Place tuna on a grill coated with nonstick vegetable spray. Cover grill and cook 5 minutes on each side. Place tuna on a plate and cut into 1/4-inch slices; keep warm.

WHEN READY TO SERVE

Heat fajita shells according to package directions. Divide the tuna, onions, and green peppers among fajita shells. Roll up and spoon tomatillo salsa over each. Garnish the top with diced tomatoes and enjoy!

297 Calories
19.6 g Protein
33.6 g Carbohydrates
9.7 g Fat
29.5% Calories from Fat
3.0 g Fiber
251 mg Sodium
23 mg Cholesterol

4 SERVINGS

This is a simple yet elegant way to serve salmon. Serve with lemon rice pilaf and a salad of baby greens dressed in a raspberry vinaigrette and accented with a small wedge of montrachet cheese.

¼ cup honey
3 tablespoons peppercorn mustard

1 salmon filet (24 ounces)

Combine honey and mustard in a small bowl.

WHEN READY TO GRILL
Brush honey and mustard mixture over top of salmon. Over hot coals, place salmon, skin side down, on a grill coated with nonstick vegetable spray. Cover grill and cook 10 to 12 minutes. Remove the skin and divide the salmon into four pieces.

316 Calories
33.3 g Protein
17.8 g Carbohydrates
11.9 g Fat
33.8% Calories from Fat
0.0 g Fiber
373 mg Sodium
90 mg Cholesterol

4 SERVINGS

My husband loves hot and spicy food and these shrimp are among his all-time favorites. Complement the meal with a first course of Louisiana gumbo and serve the shrimp with white rice, French bread, and a glass of light beer.

Marinade

½ cup fresh lemon juice
1 tablespoon extra-virgin olive oil
2 tablespoons freshly ground pepper
2 teaspoons rosemary
2 teaspoons Worcestershire sauce
1 teaspoon hot pepper sauce

2 pounds large shrimp

To make marinade

Combine lemon juice, olive oil, pepper, rosemary, Worcestershire sauce, and hot pepper sauce in a non-metal dish. Add shrimp (do not remove the shells) and toss to coat. Cover dish and refrigerate 1 hour, turning shrimp at least once.

WHEN READY TO GRILL

Place shrimp on skewers. Over hot coals, place shrimp on a grill coated with nonstick vegetable spray. Cover grill and cook 3 minutes on each side.

200 Calories
37.2 g Protein
3.3 g Carbohydrates
3.8 g Fat
16.9% Calories from Fat
0.1 g Fiber
412 mg Sodium
345 mg Cholesterol

4 SERVINGS

This is a beautiful entree that combines vegetables and fish into one dish. The Carrot Puree and jalapeño sauce can be made ahead of time and gently reheated before serving. Start the meal with Grilled Butternut Squash and Pear Soup.

Jalapeño Sauce

1 can (14.5 ounces) nonfat chicken broth

1 medium onion, minced

1 minced jalapeño*

¼ teaspoon *each* salt, garlic salt, and freshly
  ground pepper

Carrot Puree

5 new potatoes, peeled and diced

2 carrots, peeled and diced

1 small yellow onion, peeled and thinly sliced

2 small cloves garlic, minced

½ teaspoon garlic salt

¼ teaspoon *each* salt and freshly ground pepper

2 tablespoons fresh chopped chives

4 mahi-mahi filets (5 ounces each)

8 teaspoons extra-virgin olive oil

*The seeds of the jalapeño pepper are very hot. To avoid burning your skin, wear rubber or latex gloves when removing the seeds. Immediately wash the knife, cutting surface, and gloves when finished.

278 Calories
22.9 g Protein
23.8 g Carbohydrates
10.1 g Fat
32.7% Calories from Fat
2.6 g Fiber
877 mg Sodium
79 mg Cholesterol

To make Jalapeño Sauce

In a small saucepan over moderately high heat, combine broth, onions, and jalapeño. Bring to a boil and cook about 30 minutes, or until reduced to 1 cup. Add salt, garlic salt, and pepper and blend well. Cover and set aside.

To make Carrot Puree

In a large pot over moderately high heat, combine potatoes, carrots, onion, and garlic and bring to a boil. Reduce heat and simmer 30 minutes. Drain mixture and place in work bowl of food processor fitted with a metal blade and process until pureed. Add garlic salt, salt, pepper, and chives; blend well. Transfer carrot puree to bowl and cover with aluminum foil to keep it warm.

WHEN READY TO GRILL

Brush both sides of mahi-mahi with 1 teaspoon olive oil. Over hot coals, place mahi-mahi on a grill coated with non-stick vegetable spray. Cover grill and cook 4 to 5 minutes on each side.

WHEN READY TO SERVE

Spoon ½ cup Carrot Puree on a dinner plate and top with a mahi-mahi filet. Spoon about 2 tablespoons Jalapeño Sauce over each filet and garnish with parsley and a slivered carrot curl, if desired.

2 SERVINGS*

*Long hot summer days are the perfect time to enjoy this
wonderfully light and refreshing one–dish tuna salad that is so easy
to prepare and deliciously satisfying to eat. Serve with peasant bread.*

Marinade

2 tablespoons fresh lemon juice
½ tablespoon extra-virgin olive oil
⅛ teaspoon freshly ground pepper

1 yellowfin tuna filet (6 ounces)

Lemon Vinaigrette

3 tablespoons fresh lemon juice
½ tablespoon Dijon mustard
Dash *each* of salt and freshly ground pepper
3 tablespoons extra-virgin olive oil

1 red pepper
1 teaspoon extra-virgin olive oil
4 new potatoes, halved and parboiled 5 minutes
Mixed greens
2 hard-boiled eggs, cut into 8 wedges
1 tomato, cut into 8 wedges
1 tablespoon capers

*The recipe can be easily doubled to serve 4.

684 Calories
31.2 g Protein
64.3 g Carbohydrates
35.3 g Fat
46.4% Calories from Fat
4.5 g Fiber
321 mg Sodium
243 mg Cholesterol

To make marinade

Combine lemon juice, olive oil, and pepper in a non-metal dish. Add tuna and turn to coat both sides. Cover dish and refrigerate 30 minutes.

To make Lemon Vinaigrette

In work bowl of food processor fitted with a metal blade, process lemon juice, mustard, salt, and pepper until blended. In a slow steady stream, add olive oil and process until well blended.

WHEN READY TO GRILL

Over hot coals, place the red pepper on a grill coated with nonstick vegetable spray. Cover grill and cook 14 to 20 minutes, or until skin is charred all over, turning pepper as the skin blackens. Place the pepper in a plastic bag for 15 minutes. When pepper is cool enough to handle, peel away the skin and remove the top and seeds (do not rinse the pepper). Cut the pepper into strips and set aside.

Pour 1 teaspoon olive oil in a bag and place potatoes in it. Turn to coat. Thread potatoes onto skewers and place on a grill. Cover grill and cook 10 to 12 minutes or until brown and tender, turning every 3 minutes.

Place tuna on grill. Cover grill and cook the tuna 5 minutes on each side. Cool slightly and cut into $\frac{1}{4}$-inch slices.

WHEN READY TO SERVE

Arrange a layer of mixed greens on two dinner plates. Divide the tuna slices and place in the center of the lettuce. In spoke fashion, surround the tuna with sections of tomatoes, potatoes, red peppers, and eggs. Sprinkle top of each salad with 1 tablespoon capers and drizzle Lemon Vinaigrette all over.

4 SERVINGS

The monkfish is a rather homely fish to look at but the meat in the tail is exceptionally delicious. Monkfish can be sautéed or baked, but I prefer to grill it. Serve this colorful entree with Couscous and Vegetable Salad (page 88) and Grilled Carrots.

Marinade

1 cup fresh tangerine juice
¼ cup soy sauce
2 teaspoons chili oil
2 cloves garlic, minced
1 piece fresh ginger root, peeled and cut
   ¼ inch thick

1 monkfish filet (8 ounces), cut into 1-inch cubes*

Kebab Fruit and Vegetables

1 tangerine, seeded and split into 3 segments
1 red pepper, cut into eight 1-inch squares
2 green onions, cut into eight pieces each

To make marinade

Combine tangerine juice, soy sauce, chili oil, garlic, and ginger root in a nonmetal dish. Add monkfish and turn to coat. Cover dish and refrigerate for 30 minutes.

87 Calories
9.1 g Protein
8.2 g Carbohydrates
2.1 g Fat
21.7% Calories from Fat
0.8 g Fiber
527 mg Sodium
14 mg Cholesterol

WHEN READY TO GRILL
Alternate pieces of monkfish (reserve marinade), tangerine, red pepper, and green onions on skewers. Over hot coals, place monkfish kebabs on a grill coated with nonstick vegetable spray. Cover grill and cook 4 to 6 minutes, or until monkfish is no longer opaque, turning every 2 minutes and brushing with marinade.

***If monkfish is unavailable, substitute lobster.**

6 SERVINGS

The grouper is a member of the sea bass family. It has firm, white flesh and a characteristic flavor. The orange marinade infuses the fish with a delicious tangy flavor, especially when it is grilled. Serve with Zucchini and Yellow Squash Ribbons.

Marinade

½ cup *each* soy sauce and fresh orange juice
¼ cup rice wine
½ teaspoon sesame oil
¼ teaspoon crushed red pepper
2 cloves garlic, minced
1 piece fresh ginger root, peeled and cut
    ¼ inch thick

6 grouper filets (6 ounces each)*

To make marinade

Combine soy sauce, orange juice, rice wine, sesame oil, red pepper, garlic, and ginger root in a nonmetal dish. Add grouper filets and turn to coat both sides. Cover dish and refrigerate for 30 minutes.

WHEN READY TO GRILL

Over hot coals, place grouper filets, skin side up, on a grill coated with nonstick vegetable spray. Cover grill and cook 30 seconds. Turn filets over, cover grill, and cook 5 minutes, or until no longer opaque.

*If grouper is unavailable, substitute sea bass or monkfish.

273 Calories
33.9 g Protein
14.2 g Carbohydrates
4.0 g Fat
13.2% Calories from Fat
0.0 g Fiber
811 mg Sodium
74 mg Cholesterol

4 SERVINGS

*The spicy hot sauce is a melange of Chinese ingredients that accent the
subtle flavor of the marinated grilled tuna. Spoon a small amount beside the
grilled tuna and serve with steamed basmati rice and grilled Japanese Eggplant.*

Spicy Hot Sauce

5 cloves garlic
2 teaspoons finely chopped fresh ginger root
2 green onions, cut into 1-inch lengths
1 teaspoon hot bean paste*

½ cup nonfat chicken broth
2 tablespoons soy sauce
2 tablespoons rice wine
1 tablespoon black vinegar
1 tablespoon honey
¼ teaspoon sesame oil
1½ teaspoons cornstarch

Marinade

3 tablespoons rice wine
1 piece fresh ginger root, peeled and cut
    ¼ inch thick
2 green onions, thinly sliced
1 tablespoon soy sauce
½ teaspoon sesame oil

297 Calories
37.7 g Protein
13.1 g Carbohydrates
8.5 g Fat
25.8% Calories from Fat
0.4 g Fiber
963 mg Sodium
60 mg Cholesterol

4 tuna steaks (6 ounces each)

***Hot bean paste, rice wine, black vinegar, and sesame oil are
available in most Asian food stores.**

To make Spicy Hot Sauce

Combine garlic, ginger root, green onions, and hot bean paste in work bowl of food processor fitted with a metal blade and process until smooth.

Combine chicken broth, soy sauce, rice wine, black vinegar, honey, and sesame oil in a small bowl. Add cornstarch and blend well.

Coat the bottom of a small, heavy saucepan with a nonstick vegetable spray and place it over moderately high heat. When pan is hot, add hot bean paste mixture and cook 20 seconds. Add chicken broth mixture, blend, and bring to a boil. Cook 20 seconds or until mixture is thick. Set aside in a covered container.

To make marinade

Combine rice wine, ginger root, green onions, soy sauce, and sesame oil in a nonmetal dish. Add tuna steaks and turn to coat both sides. Cover dish and refrigerate 30 minutes.

WHEN READY TO GRILL
Over hot coals, place tuna steaks on a grill coated with nonstick vegetable spray. Cover grill and cook 5 minutes on each side.

WHEN READY TO SERVE
Place tuna steaks on individual dinner plates. Garnish each serving with Spicy Hot Sauce on the side.

4 SERVINGS

This is an unusual dish that combines the marvelous flavors of grilled eggplant and seafood, both of which are served on a bed of fettuccini and topped with a piquant Grilled Red Pepper Sauce. Serve with a mixed green salad and crusty peasant bread.

Grilled Red Pepper Sauce

3 red peppers

1 large clove garlic, minced

1½ tablespoons *each* sherry vinegar and
    extra-virgin olive oil

¼ teaspoon plus a pinch of cayenne

1 eggplant (14 ounces), sliced ¼ inch thick

Salt

1½ tablespoons extra-virgin olive oil

¾ pound medium shrimp, shells removed

¾ pound sea scallops

12 ounces fresh fettuccini, cooked according to
    package directions

WHEN READY TO GRILL

Over hot coals, place the peppers on a grill coated with nonstick vegetable spray. Cover grill and cook peppers 14 to 20 minutes, or until skins are charred all over, turning peppers as skins blacken. Place the peppers in a plastic bag for 15 minutes. When peppers are cool enough to handle, peel away the skin and remove the top and seeds (do not rinse the peppers).

509 Calories
37.0 g Protein
59.1 g Carbohydrates
13.8 g Fat
24.5% Calories from Fat
4.0 g Fiber
291 mg Sodium
221 mg Cholesterol

To make Red Pepper Sauce

In work bowl of food processor fitted with a metal blade, process garlic until chopped. Add peppers and process until smooth. Add sherry vinegar, olive oil, and cayenne and process until well blended. Keep warm until ready to serve. (The sauce can be made a day ahead and refrigerated in a covered container overnight.)

When ready to serve, warm in a heavy saucepan over moderate heat, stirring occasionally.

Place eggplant in a colander and sprinkle the slices with salt. Set aside for 30 minutes. Remove eggplant slices from colander and place in a plastic bag with ½ tablespoon of the olive oil. Toss eggplant in olive oil to coat all over.

Pour the other 1 tablespoon olive oil in a plastic bag and add shrimp and scallops; turn to coat. Thread the shrimps and scallops on skewers.

WHEN READY TO GRILL

Over hot coals, place the shrimp and scallop skewers along with the eggplant on grill. Cover grill and cook the shrimp and scallops for 3 minutes on each side and the eggplant for 4 to 5 minutes on each side, or until brown and tender. Set aside and keep warm.

Prepare fettuccini according to package directions. Drain well.

WHEN READY TO SERVE

Remove skin and cut eggplant into small cubes. Divide fettuccini among dinner plates. Distribute the shrimp, scallops, and eggplant over the fettuccini. Spoon Grilled Red Pepper sauce over the top. Sprinkle with finely chopped parsley, if desired.

4 SERVINGS

*The peach jam glaze imparts a wonderfully rich flavor to the shrimp
once it is grilled. Serve with Grilled Peaches and lemon rice pilaf.*

Marinade
¼ cup peach jam
2 tablespoons tamari
¼ teaspoon crushed red pepper

24 large shrimp, peeled

Kebab Fruit and Vegetables
3 fresh peaches, cut into 8 wedges
4 green onions, cut into eight 2-inch lengths
1 red pepper, cut into 8 cubes

To make marinade
Combine peach jam, tamari, and red pepper in a small saucepan over moderate heat. Cook 4 minutes, stirring occasionally. When the marinade comes to room temperature, add shrimp and turn to coat all over.

WHEN READY TO GRILL
Alternate pieces of shrimp (reserve marinade), peach, green onion, and red pepper among skewers. Place shrimp over hot coals on a grill coated with nonstick vegetable spray. Cover grill and cook 3 minutes on each side, brushing with marinade every 1 to 2 minutes.

214 Calories
26.8 g Protein
24.2 g Carbohydrates
1.4 g Fat
5.9% Calories from Fat
1.8 g Fiber
773 mg Sodium
232 mg Cholesterol

4 SERVINGS

The recipe for the Mustard Dill Sauce comes from my good friend, Sugar.
The Dijon mustard and dill combination nicely complements the flavor of the grilled
salmon. Serve with Zucchini and Yellow Squash Ribbons and lemon rice pilaf.

Sugar's Mustard Dill Sauce

⅓ cup lowfat mayonnaise
2 heaping tablespoons Dijon mustard
1 teaspoon minced fresh dill
1 tablespoon sugar (or 1 packet sugar substitute)
Onion powder or fresh lemon juice, to taste
  (optional)

4 salmon filets (6 ounces each)
4 teaspoons extra-virgin olive oil
Salt and pepper
4 sprigs of dill (optional)

To make Sugar's Mustard Dill Sauce

Combine mayonnaise, mustard, dill, sugar, and optional onion powder or lemon juice and blend well. Refrigerate, covered, until ready to use.

WHEN READY TO GRILL

Brush each salmon filet with 1 teaspoon olive oil and lightly sprinkle with salt and pepper. Over hot coals, place salmon filets, skin side down, on a grill coated with nonstick vegetable spray. Cover grill and cook 10 minutes.

WHEN READY TO SERVE

Discard salmon skin. Place salmon filets on individual dinner plates and top each with 2 tablespoons Sugar's Mustard Dill Sauce. Garnish with a sprig of dill, if desired.

385 Calories
36.8 g Protein
4.6 g Carbohydrates
23.3 g Fat
54.4% Calories from Fat
0.0 g Fiber
341 mg Sodium
115 mg Cholesterol

4 SERVINGS

Wrapping the salmon in grape leaves allows it to remain exceptionally moist throughout the grilling process. Serve with rice pilaf mixed with raisins and toasted pinenuts and a Greek salad (page 108).

Marinade
$\frac{1}{4}$ cup fresh lemon juice
1 tablespoon extra-virgin olive oil
1 clove garlic, minced
$\frac{1}{4}$ teaspoon freshly ground white pepper

10 (or more) grape leaves, rinsed
1 salmon filet ($1\frac{1}{2}$ pounds)

2 tablespoons diced red pepper
4 Greek olives, diced
3 tablespoons diced roma tomato
1 tablespoon minced parsley
$\frac{1}{4}$ teaspoon red wine vinegar
Dash of marjoram

278 Calories
32.7 g Protein
2.7 g Carbohydrates
14.5 g Fat
46.9% Calories from Fat
0.3 g Fiber
136 mg Sodium
90 mg Cholesterol

To make marinade

Combine lemon juice, olive oil, garlic, and pepper in a nonmetal dish. Add salmon and turn to coat both sides, ending with skin side up. Cover dish and refrigerate for 30 minutes.

Place about 6 to 8 (or more, if needed) grape leaves, slightly overlapping each other, on a work surface. Place salmon, skin side down, on top of leaves. Cover salmon with remaining leaves and bring bottom leaves up and around salmon to enclose it.

WHEN READY TO GRILL

Over hot coals, place salmon on a grilling grid coated with nonstick vegetable spray. Cover grill and cook 20 to 22 minutes, or until salmon is no longer pink when a grape leaf is pulled away from the salmon and a knife is inserted into center.

While salmon is cooking, combine red pepper, olives, tomatoes, parsley, red wine vinegar, and marjoram in a small bowl.

WHEN READY TO SERVE

Remove salmon from grape leaves. Cut salmon into four pieces (discard skin) and place on individual dinner plates. Top each filet with 2 tablespoons vegetable mixture.

4 SERVINGS

Saffron is a very expensive seasoning made from the stigmas of the crocus salivus. *Each flower produces only three stigmas which are dried and later made into saffron powder. It requires at least 5,000 flowers to yield enough stigmas to make one ounce of saffron powder. As you will taste from this recipe, it is definitely worth the trouble.*

4 salmon filets (6 ounces each)
Salt and pepper
3 tablespoons fresh lemon juice

Saffron Sauce
⅓ cup finely chopped shallots
3 tablespoons white wine
½ cup clam juice
⅛ teaspoon saffron
3 tablespoons light margarine
1 tablespoon nondairy cream
⅛ teaspoon *each* salt and freshly ground pepper
¼ cup frozen peas, defrosted

Place salmon in a nonmetal dish. Sprinkle with salt and pepper and pour lemon juice on top. Cover dish and refrigerate for 30 minutes.

295 Calories
33.3 g Protein
4.0 g Carbohydrates
15.0 g Fat
45.6% Calories from Fat
0.3 g Fiber
258 mg Sodium
90 mg Cholesterol

To make Saffron Sauce

Coat a small heavy saucepan with vegetable spray and place over moderate heat for 1 minute. Add shallots and cook 2 minutes, stirring occasionally. Add wine, increase heat to high, and cook 2 minutes, or until wine has been reduced to 1 tablespoon. Add clam juice and saffron and cook over moderately low heat for 5 minutes. Remove saucepan from heat; add margarine, 1 tablespoon at a time, and stir to blend. Add cream, salt, pepper, and peas and blend well. Keep warm over very low heat.

WHEN READY TO GRILL

Over hot coals, place salmon, skin side down, on a grill coated with nonstick vegetable spray. Cover grill and cook 10 minutes.

WHEN READY TO SERVE

Discard salmon skin. Spoon about 2 to 3 tablespoons Saffron Sauce on each dinner plate and top with a salmon filet. Garnish each serving with a sprig of fresh parsley.

4 SERVINGS

The sweetness of the sea bass laced with Ginger Oil contrasts nicely with the Spicy Black Bean Sauce. Serve with lemon rice pilaf and a fresh fruit salad.

Black Bean Sauce

1 tablespoon canola oil

½ teaspoon sesame oil

1 teaspoon *each* minced garlic, ginger root, and
    Bermuda onion

1 teaspoon fermented black beans*

2 green onions, julienned

1 carrot, julienned

1 cup chicken broth

1 tablespoon cornstarch dissolved in
    1½ tablespoons cold water

2 sea bass filets (12 ounces each)

4 teaspoons Ginger Oil (page 186)

*Fermented black beans are available in most Asian food stores.

273 Calories
34.0 g Protein
5.3 g Carbohydrates
12.2 g Fat
7.8% Calories from Fat
0.8 g Fiber
387 mg Sodium
74 mg Cholesterol

To make Black Bean Sauce

Heat canola oil and sesame oil in a medium saucepan over moderately high heat. Add garlic, ginger root, onion, and black beans and cook 1 minute, stirring frequently. Add green onions and carrot and cook 1 minute. Add chicken broth and dissolved cornstarch and cook until sauce thickens. Keep warm.

WHEN READY TO GRILL

Brush each side of sea bass with 1 teaspoon Ginger Oil. Over hot coals, place sea bass on a grill coated with non-stick vegetable spray. Cover grill and cook 5 to 6 minutes on each side.

WHEN READY TO SERVE

Cut each sea bass filet into 2 pieces. Divide the sea bass filets among 4 dinner plates. Surround each serving with Black Bean Sauce.

4 SERVINGS

*Sea scallops are members of the mollusk family and are
known for their two shells that are beautifully scalloped. The edible
part of the scallop is the abductor muscle, or eye, which opens and closes
the shells. Serve this delicious entree with steamed broccoli and a fresh fruit salad.*

WHEN READY TO GRILL
Place 6 to 8 scallops on each skewer. Over hot coals, place scallop kebabs on a grill coated with nonstick vegetable spray. Cover grill and cook 3 to 5 minutes on each side.

Marinade
$\frac{1}{4}$ cup *each* rice wine and soy sauce
1 tablespoon sugar
1 piece fresh ginger root, peeled and cut
    $\frac{1}{4}$ inch thick

$1\frac{1}{2}$ pounds sea scallops

To make marinade
In a small saucepan over moderate heat, combine rice wine, soy sauce, sugar, and ginger root and blend well. Bring to a boil, lower heat, and simmer for 20 minutes, stirring occasionally. Remove ginger root. Allow marinade to come to room temperature. Use the marinade immediately or refrigerate in a covered container for up to 4 weeks.

Place scallops in a nonmetal dish and add $\frac{1}{4}$ cup marinade; turn scallops to coat both sides. Cover dish and refrigerate 45 minutes.

154 Calories
23.8 g Protein
9 6 g Carbohydrates
1.0 g Fat
6.1% Calories from Fat
0.0 g Fiber
1248 mg Sodium
45 mg Cholesterol

6 SERVINGS

The shrimp combine nicely with the Asian marinade and the flavor is heightened after grilling. Serve with Grilled Pears and herbed rice.

Marinade

¼ cup *each* rice wine and soy sauce

1 tablespoon sugar

1 piece fresh ginger root, peeled and cut
   ¼ inch thick

4 teaspoons sesame seeds

2 pounds large shrimp, peeled and deveined

To make marinade

In a small saucepan over moderate heat, combine rice wine, soy sauce, sugar, and ginger root and blend well. Bring to a boil, lower heat, and simmer for 20 minutes, stirring occasionally. Remove ginger root. Add sesame seeds and allow marinade to come to room temperature.

Place shrimp in a nonmetal dish and pour marinade over top; turn shrimp to coat pieces. Cover dish and refrigerate up to 2 hours.

WHEN READY TO GRILL

Place shrimp on skewers by alternating the direction the heads and tails face each other. Over hot coals, place shrimp on a grill coated with nonstick vegetable spray. Cover grill and cook 3 minutes on each side.

219 Calories
37.8 g Protein
6.5 g Carbohydrates
3.4 g Fat
13.9% Calories from Fat
0.1 g Fiber
653 mg Sodium
345 mg Cholesterol

4 SERVINGS

This is a colorful entree with no limit to the kinds of fruits and vegetables you use to make up the kebabs. It presents a delicious combination of flavors and texture. Serve with grilled Pineapple Rings and steamed basmati rice.

Marinade

1 cup pineapple juice

¼ cup soy sauce

1½ tablespoons honey

1 tablespoon cornstarch

½ tablespoon toasted sesame seeds*

½ teaspoon sesame oil

1 piece fresh ginger root, peeled and sliced
    ¼ inch thick

1½ pounds large shrimp, peeled and deveined

Kebab Vegetables and Fruit

1 green pepper, cut into eight 1-inch pieces

8 cherry tomatoes

8 fresh pineapple chunks, cut into 1-inch cubes

8 mushroom caps

*To toast sesame seeds, place sesame seeds in a pan and bake in a 350° oven for 10 to 15 minutes, or until golden brown.

225 Calories
30.7 g Protein
19.2 g Carbohydrates
3.1 g Fat
12.4% Calories from Fat
2.0 g Fiber
826 mg Sodium
266 mg Cholesterol

To make marinade

In a medium saucepan over moderate heat, combine pineapple juice, soy sauce, honey, cornstarch, sesame seeds, sesame oil, and ginger root and bring to a boil, stirring occasionally. Boil 1 minute. Remove saucepan from heat and let marinade come to room temperature. (Marinade can be made several hours ahead. Store in a covered container.)

Place shrimp in a nonmetal dish and pour marinade on top. Toss shrimp to coat both sides. Cover dish and refrigerate 30 minutes.

WHEN READY TO GRILL

Alternate shrimp, pepper, tomatoes, pineapple, and mushrooms among 8 skewers. Over hot coals, place shrimp on a grill coated with nonstick vegetable spray. Cover grill and cook 3 minutes on each side.

4 SERVINGS

*The highly spiced salsa is a fusion of garlic, parsley,
and pepper. Its piquant tang balances the subtle flavor of the swordfish.
Serve with sautéed new potatoes and Grilled Asparagus.*

Garlic and Pepper Oil
½ cup extra-virgin olive oil
4 cloves garlic, minced
1 tablespoon freshly ground pepper

Parsley Salsa
½ cup parsley, tightly packed
2 cloves garlic
1 tablespoon capers
1 tablespoon Dijon mustard
2 tablespoons extra-virgin olive oil
¼ teaspoon *each* salt and freshly ground pepper

4 swordfish steaks (6 ounces each)
4 teaspoons Garlic and Pepper Oil

265 Calories
31.3 g Protein
1.1 g Carbohydrates
14.4 g Fat
48.9% Calories from Fat
0.2 g Fiber
287 mg Sodium
61 mg Cholesterol

To make Garlic and Pepper Oil

Combine ½ cup olive oil, 4 minced garlic cloves, and 1 tablespoon pepper in a small heavy saucepan over moderate heat and bring to a boil. Remove saucepan from heat, cover, and let Garlic and Pepper Oil sit for 30 minutes. Pour garlic and pepper oil into a glass jar with a tight-fitting lid and store in a dark, cool place. Use as needed. Makes ½ cup.

To make Parsley Salsa

In work bowl of food processor fitted with a metal blade, process parsley and garlic until finely chopped. Add capers, mustard, olive oil, salt, and pepper and process until smooth. Set aside.

WHEN READY TO GRILL

Brush each swordfish steak with ½ teaspoon garlic and pepper oil. Over hot coals, place swordfish, oiled side down, on a grill coated with nonstick vegetable spray. Brush tops of each swordfish with ½ teaspoon Garlic and Pepper Oil, cover, and cook 5 to 6 minutes on each side.

WHEN READY TO GRILL

Place swordfish steaks on individual dinner plates and garnish each serving with a table-spoon of Parsley Salsa on the side.

4 SERVINGS

The flesh of the swordfish is very meaty—making it perfect for grilling. The subtle flavor of the marinade complements any vegetables: the choice and variety are a matter of personal preference. Serve with grilled Greek Vegetables and Saffron Rice.

Marinade
½ cup fresh lemon juice
1 tablespoon extra-virgin olive oil
1 clove garlic, minced
1 bay leaf
1 teaspoon oregano
½ teaspoon freshly ground pepper
⅛ teaspoon *each* salt and cayenne

1½ pounds swordfish, cut into 1½-inch cubes

Saffron Rice
1 tablespoon extra-virgin olive oil
1 large Vidalia onion, chopped
4 large cloves garlic, minced
1 can (14½ ounces) fatfree chicken broth
¼ teaspoon saffron
1 cup arborio rice

⅛ teaspoon *each* salt and freshly ground pepper

Kebab Vegetables
1 red pepper, cut into 1-inch squares
1 zucchini, cut into ¼ inch thick slices

239 Calories
31.8 g Protein
5.5 g Carbohydrates
9.8 g Fat
36.8% Calories from Fat
0.8 g Fiber
208 mg Sodium
61 mg Cholesterol

To make marinade

Combine lemon juice, olive oil, garlic, bay leaf, oregano, pepper, salt, and cayenne in a nonmetal dish. Add swordfish and turn to coat both sides. Cover dish and refrigerate 30 minutes.

To make Saffron Rice

Coat the bottom of a medium saucepan with nonstick vegetable spray. Add olive oil and place over moderate heat for 1 minute. Add onions and garlic and cook over moderately low heat for 30 minutes, or until golden brown, stirring occasionally.

Combine chicken broth and saffron in a medium saucepan and bring to a boil over moderate heat. Add rice and cook, covered, for 15 minutes over low heat, or until all of the liquid has been absorbed. Add onion mixture, salt, and pepper and blend well. Keep warm.

WHEN READY TO GRILL

Alternate pieces of swordfish (reserving marinade), pepper, and zucchini on skewers. Over hot coals, place swordfish on a grill coated with nonstick vegetable spray. Cover grill and cook 8 to 10 minutes, turning skewers every 3 minutes, brushing swordfish and vegetables with marinade. The fish is done when the flesh is opaque and can be easily pierced with a fork.

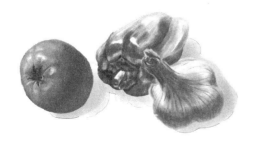

4 SERVINGS

The combination of fish and a fruity salsa is a refreshing blend of tastes and textures. Serve with Saffron Rice (page 224) and Fruit Kebabs.

Salsa

1 cup *each* diced pineapple, mango, and tomato
1 tablespoon fresh lime juice
½ tablespoon honey
1 teaspoon *each* rice vinegar and soy sauce
2 jalapeños, seeded and minced*

Fiery Hot Pepper Oil

½ cup extra-virgin olive oil
2 tablespoons crushed red pepper

4 swordfish filets (6 ounces each)

*The seeds of jalapeño peppers are very hot. To avoid burning your skin, wear rubber or latex gloves when removing the seeds. Immediately wash the knife, cutting surface, and gloves when finished.

297 Calories
32.2 g Protein
17.5 g Carbohydrates
11.0 g Fat
33.4% Calories from Fat
2.1 g Fiber
229 mg Sodium
61 mg Cholesterol

To make Salsa

Combine pineapple, mango, tomato, lime juice, honey, rice vinegar, soy sauce, and jalapeños in a small non-metal bowl and blend well. Cover bowl and refrigerate pineapple salsa for up to 4 hours.

To make Fiery Hot Pepper Oil

Combine oil and red pepper in a small heavy saucepan over moderate heat and bring to a boil. Remove saucepan from heat, cover, and let sit for 30 minutes. Pour pepper oil into a glass jar with a tight-fitting lid and store in a dark place. Use as needed. Makes ½ cup.

WHEN READY TO GRILL

Brush each swordfish filet with ½ teaspoon Fiery Hot Pepper Oil. Place filets, oiled side down, on a grill coated with nonstick vegetable spray. Brush top of each filet with ½ teaspoon Fiery Hot Pepper Oil. Cover grill and cook swordfish for 5 minutes on each side.

WHEN READY TO GRILL

Place swordfish filets on individual dinner plates. Spoon pineapple salsa beside each serving.

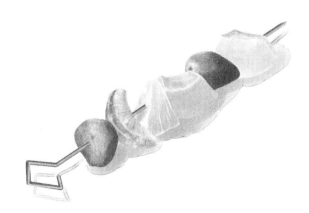

4 SERVINGS

Wasabi paste (horseradish) is a condiment used in Japanese cooking and is found in Asian food stores. Because it is very hot, I like to use only a small amount in the marinade. If you like your food very hot, try adding a little more, but in very small increments. Serve with Papaya Salsa as a garnish and steamed brown basmati rice and grilled Vegetable Melange.

Papaya Salsa

$\frac{1}{2}$ cup papaya, peeled and seeded and cut into $\frac{1}{4}$-inch dice

2 tablespoons *each* minced Bermuda onion and tomato

1 tablespoon fresh lime juice

1 tablespoon chopped fresh mint

2 jalapeños, minced*

Marinade

2 tablespoons *each* rice vinegar and soy sauce

1 tablespoon rice wine

$\frac{1}{2}$ teaspoon wasabi paste

$\frac{1}{2}$ teaspoon sesame oil

2 cloves garlic, minced

1 piece fresh ginger root, peeled and cut $\frac{1}{4}$ inch thick

4 yellow fin tuna steaks (6 ounces each)

*The seeds of jalapeño peppers are very hot. To avoid burning your skin, wear rubber or latex gloves when removing the seeds. Immediately wash the knife, cutting surface, and gloves when finished.

287 Calories
37.4 g Protein
10.8 g Carbohydrates
8.2 g Fat
25.9% Calories from Fat
0.7 g Fiber
579 mg Sodium
60 mg Cholesterol

To make Papaya Salsa

Combine papaya, onion, tomato, lime juice, mint, and jalapeños in a small bowl and blend well. Refrigerate, covered, up to 4 hours.

To make marinade

Combine rice vinegar, soy sauce, rice wine, wasabi paste, sesame oil, garlic, and ginger root in a nonmetal dish. Add tuna and turn to coat both sides. Cover dish and refrigerate 30 minutes.

WHEN READY TO GRILL

Over hot coals, place tuna steaks on a grill coated with nonstick vegetable spray. Cover grill and cook 5 minutes on each side.

WHEN READY TO SERVE

Place tuna steaks on individual dinner plates and accompany each serving with Papaya Salsa. Garnish salsa with a sprig of fresh mint, if desired.

4 SERVINGS

You will want to use this outstanding Honey Dijon Sauce with other kinds of grilled fish as well. Its sweet flavor delicately balances the smoky taste of the fish. Serve with grilled Pineapple Rings and stuffed zucchini.

WHEN READY TO SERVE

Remove ginger root from Honey Dijon Sauce. Place one shark steak on each dinner plate and spoon 2 tablespoons of sauce over each. Garnish each serving with chopped chives, if desired.

Honey Dijon Sauce

3 tablespoons *each* honey and plain nonfat yogurt
1 tablespoon hoisin sauce
1½ teaspoons *each* Dijon mustard and soy sauce
1½ tablespoons chopped chives
1 piece fresh ginger root, peeled and cut
  ¼ inch thick

8 teaspoons Ginger Oil (page 186)
4 shark steaks* (6 ounces each)

To make Honey Dijon Sauce

Combine honey, yogurt, hoisin sauce, mustard, soy sauce, chives, and ginger root in a small bowl. Set aside.

Soak 1 cup of your favorite smoking wood chips in water for 30 minutes.

WHEN READY TO GRILL

Place wet smoking chips on hot coals. Brush one side of each shark steak with 1 teaspoon Ginger Oil and place over coals, oiled side down, on a grill coated with nonstick vegetable spray. Brush top of each steak with 1 teaspoon Ginger Oil, cover grill, and cook 5 minutes on each side.

*If shark is unavailable, substitute tuna, salmon, or swordfish.

345 Calories
29.1 g Protein
21.5 g Carbohydrates
15.8 g Fat
41.3% Calories from Fat
0.8 g Fiber
1001 mg Sodium
62 mg Cholesterol

VEGETABLES

4 SERVINGS

Asparagus never tasted so good!

1 pound asparagus
1 tablespoon extra-virgin olive oil
Dash of freshly ground white pepper

Snap off the ends of the asparagus. Place asparagus in a plastic bag and add olive oil. Roll asparagus in the olive oil until well coated.

WHEN READY TO GRILL
Over hot coals, place asparagus on a grilling grid coated with nonstick vegetable spray. Cover grill and cook 8 to 10 minutes, or until lightly browned, turning occasionally. Sprinkle asparagus with white pepper before serving.

43 Calories
1.5 g Protein
2.4 g Carbohydrates
3.6 g Fat
74.7% Calories from Fat
0.5 g Fiber
7 mg Sodium
0 mg Cholesterol

6 SERVINGS

*Whether you are a vegetarian or not, you will agree that this
savory dish is the highlight of any meal. The grilled vegetables mingle
perfectly with the spices and other ingredients to create a sensational flavor.
Serve on a bed of brown basmati rice and top with Raita (page 124).*

1 eggplant ($\frac{1}{2}$ pound), cut into $\frac{1}{2}$-inch slices
10 new potatoes, halved
2 carrots, cut into $1\frac{1}{2}$-inch chunks
1 crookneck squash, cut into $1\frac{1}{2}$-inch chunks
1 Bermuda onion, cut into wedges
1 red pepper
2 tablespoons extra-virgin olive oil
$\frac{2}{3}$ cup apple juice
$\frac{1}{2}$ cup garbanzo beans
1 apple, peeled and cut into 1-inch chunks
$\frac{1}{2}$ cup raisins
1 tablespoon curry powder
$\frac{3}{4}$ teaspoon cumin
$\frac{1}{2}$ teaspoon cinnamon

Sprinkle the eggplant with salt and place in a colander for 30 minutes.

Place potatoes, carrots, squash, and onion in a plastic bag. Pour oil over vegetables and turn to coat pieces. Place vegetables on skewers and set aside.

349 Calories
7.0 g Protein
71.6 g Carbohydrates
5.6 g Fat
14.4% Calories from Fat
5.5 g Fiber
36 mg Sodium
0 mg Cholesterol

WHEN READY TO GRILL

Over hot coals, place the red pepper on a grill coated with nonstick vegetable spray. Cover grill and cook 14 to 20 minutes, or until skin is charred all over, turning pepper as skin blackens. Place pepper in a plastic bag for 15 minutes. When the pepper is cool enough to handle, peel away the skin and remove the top and seeds (do not rinse the pepper). Cut the pepper into strips and set aside.

Place eggplant slices and vegetable skewers on grill. Cover grill and cook 10 to 12 minutes, turning vegetables every 3 minutes.

Remove skin and cut eggplant into cubes. Place eggplant, potatoes, carrots, squash, onion, red pepper, apple juice, garbanzo beans, apple, raisins, curry powder, cumin, and cinnamon in a large saucepan over moderate heat and blend well. Bring to a boil, reduce heat, cover, and simmer 7 to 10 minutes, or until heated through.

4 SERVINGS

*Acorn squash can be served with just a sprinkling of brown sugar
or is equally delicious filled with Fruited Brown Rice and Quinoa.*

2 acorn squash
4 teaspoons extra-virgin olive oil

Fruited Brown Rice and Quinoa
½ cup water
¼ cup brown rice
½ cup water
¼ cup quinoa
2 tablespoons light margarine
½ cup chopped onions
½ cup diced apple
¼ cup raisins
¼ teaspoon *each* cinnamon and powdered ginger
⅛ teaspoon white pepper

232 Calories
3.8 g Protein
36.7 g Carbohydrates
9.1 g Fat
35.2% Calories from Fat
4.9 g Fiber
76 mg Sodium
0 mg Cholesterol

*Analysis reflects acorn squash filled with Fruited Brown Rice and Quinoa.

Cut the acorn squash in half and remove the seeds. Brush each half with 1 teaspoon olive oil.

WHEN READY TO GRILL
Over hot coals, place squash (cut side down) on a grill coated with nonstick vegetable spray. Cover grill and cook 20 minutes on each side or until tender.

To make Fruited Brown Rice and Quinoa

In 2 separate small saucepans, bring water to a boil over moderately high heat. Add brown rice to one saucepan and quinoa to the other, cover, and cook over low heat for 20 minutes.

Melt margarine in a medium saucepan over moderate heat. Add chopped onions and cook 5 minutes, stirring occasionally. Add brown rice, quinoa, apple, raisins, cinnamon, ginger, and white pepper and blend well. Spoon into grilled acorn squash halves.

4 SERVINGS

Naturally mild Bermuda onions acquire a distinctly sweet flavor when grilled.

2 tablespoons extra-virgin olive oil
1 tablespoon minced garlic
3 tablespoons chopped fresh dill
½ teaspoon freshly ground pepper

2 Bermuda onions, peeled and quartered

Combine olive oil, garlic, dill, and pepper in a medium bowl. Add onion, one quarter at a time, and turn to coat all over. Place 4 onion quarters on each skewer.

WHEN READY TO GRILL
Over hot coals, place onions on a grill coated with non-stick vegetable spray. Cover grill and cook 10 to 12 minutes, or until onions are golden brown on the outside and soft inside, turning onions every 3 minutes.

97 Calories
1.3 g Protein
8.2 g Carbohydrates
6.9 g Fat
64.1% Calories from Fat
1.4 g Fiber
2 mg Sodium
0 mg Cholesterol

4 SERVINGS

*Cooking carrots on the grill heightens the flavor
and sweetness of these wonderful vegetables.*

8 carrots
4 teaspoons Fiery Hot Pepper Oil (page 226)

WHEN READY TO GRILL
Brush each carrot with ½ teaspoon Fiery Hot Pepper Oil.
Over hot coals, place carrots on a grill coated with nonstick vegetable spray. Cover grill and cook carrots for 10 to
12 minutes, or until tender and browned, turning carrots
every 4 minutes.

104 Calories
1.6 g Protein
15.1 g Carbohydrates
4.7 g Fat
40.9% Calories from Fat
2.2 g Fiber
96 mg Sodium
0 mg Cholesterol

6 (1-CUP) SERVINGS

The smoky accent from the grill in combination with the flavors of the butternut squash, pear, and herbs is sensational in this versatile soup. It can be enjoyed warm or cold. Serve with your favorite cornbread.

1 butternut squash (1 pound)
1 pear, halved, seeds and stem removed
1 can (14½ ounces) fatfree chicken broth
1 medium onion, coarsely chopped
2 medium shallots, coarsely chopped
½ teaspoon thyme
¼ teaspoon *each* rosemary, salt, and freshly
   ground pepper
6 tablespoons skimmed evaporated milk
Lowfat sour cream (optional)
Chopped chives (optional)

Preheat oven to 325°

   Cut squash in half and remove seeds. Place squash on a baking sheet coated with vegetable spray and bake for 35 minutes.

88 Calories
3.4 g Protein
18.9 g Carbohydrates
0.9 g Fat
9.1% Calories from Fat
4.2 g Fiber
406 mg Sodium
1 mg Cholesterol

WHEN READY TO GRILL

Over hot coals, place squash and pear halves on a grill coated with nonstick vegetable spray. Cover grill and cook 4 to 5 minutes on each side.

Scoop out flesh from squash and combine it in a large saucepan over moderately high heat with chicken broth, pear, onions, shallots, thyme, rosemary, salt, and pepper. Bring to a boil, cover, and simmer 20 minutes. Remove saucepan from heat and allow to sit for 10 minutes.

Transfer soup mixture to work bowl of food processor fitted with a metal blade and process until pureed. Return soup mixture to saucepan and add evaporated milk, blending well. If serving hot, serve immediately and garnish each serving with a dollop of lowfat sour cream sprinkled with chopped chives, if desired. If serving the soup chilled, refrigerate, covered, for several hours or overnight.

6 (½-CUP) SERVINGS

Caponata is an Italian eggplant and onion dish that is most commonly prepared directly on a stove. By grilling the vegetables first, they acquire a delicious smoky flavor that is highlighted by the other ingredients. This versatile dish can be served as an appetizer on toast points, as a salad on a bed of lettuce, or stuffed in whole wheat pita bread topped with Lemon Dill Yogurt Sauce (page 4).

1 eggplant (1 pound), sliced ½ inch thick
1 Bermuda onion, cut into 4 wedges
1½ tablespoons extra-virgin olive oil
1 cup chopped celery
3 roma tomatoes, diced

2½ tablespoons red wine vinegar
1 tablespoon *each* capers and raisins
4 Greek olives (*kalamatas*), pitted and sliced
2 teaspoons sugar
¼ teaspoon freshly ground pepper

Sprinkle eggplant slices with salt and place in a colander for 30 minutes.

83 Calories
1.3 g Protein
11.6 g Carbohydrates
4.4 g Fat
47.4% Calories from Fat
1.7 g Fiber
92 mg Sodium
0 mg Cholesterol

WHEN READY TO GRILL

Place onion wedges on a skewer. Brush the onions and both sides of the eggplant slices with olive oil. Over hot coals, place eggplant and onions on a grill coated with nonstick vegetable spray. Cover grill and cook eggplant for 4 to 5 minutes on each side and the onions for 10 to 12 minutes, turning onions every 4 minutes. Remove onions from skewers and thinly slice. Remove skin and cut eggplant into cubes. Set aside.

Coat a large saucepan with nonstick vegetable spray and place over moderate heat for 1 minute. Add celery and cook 5 minutes. Add tomatoes, eggplant, onions, red wine vinegar, capers, raisins, olives, sugar, and pepper and blend well. Cook over moderately low heat for 10 minutes, or until heated through. Allow the Caponata to come to room temperature before storing it in a covered container. Refrigerate for several hours or overnight. Serve the Caponata chilled or at room temperature.

4 SERVINGS

By cooking the corn in its own husk, it remains juicy and sweet.
Surprisingly, even with the husk intact, the smoky flavor permeates the corn.

4 ears of corn

Gently peel back, but do not detach, the layers of husk on each corn, and remove the exposed fine threads. Remove one of the outer pieces of each husk to use as a string and set aside. Gently return the remaining husk to its original shape around the corn, twisting it at the top. Secure the twisted top by tying the reserved husk around it. Soak the corn in cold water for 1 hour; drain.

WHEN READY TO GRILL
Over hot coals, place the corn on a grill. Cover the grill and cook 25 to 30 minutes, turning the corn occasionally.

83 Calories
2.6 g Protein
19.3 g Carbohydrates
1.0 g Fat
10.6% Calories from Fat
2.9 g Fiber
13 mg Sodium
0 mg Cholesterol

4 SERVINGS

Crookneck squash is bright yellow, 5 to 7 inches long, and is available in the summer.

2 crookneck squash, cut in half lengthwise
2 teaspoons Fiery Hot Pepper Oil (page 226)

WHEN READY TO GRILL
Brush each side of squash with ½ teaspoon Fiery Hot Pepper Oil. Over hot coals, place squash on a grill coated with nonstick vegetable spray. Cover grill and cook squash 6 to 7 minutes on both sides, or until brown and tender.

33 Calories
0.8 g Protein
2.8 g Carbohydrates
2.4 g Fat
65.9% Calories from Fat
0.7 g Fiber
2 mg Sodium
0 mg Cholesterol

8 SERVINGS

*Grilling eggplant and zucchini enhances the true flavors of these vegetables.
In combination with roasted red peppers and onions, this becomes a truly savory
dish. Serve with grilled chicken or beef and a salad of mixed greens and tomatoes.*

2 eggplants (1 pound each), cut ½ inch thick
2 red peppers
4 tablespoons extra-virgin olive oil
2 zucchini (8 ounces each), halved
2 large onions, quartered
2 cloves garlic, minced
2 pounds tomatoes, cut ¼ inch thick and halved
½ teaspoon *each* thyme and savory
¼ teaspoon *each* salt and pepper
½ cup dry plain bread crumbs

Sprinkle eggplant slices with salt and place in a colander for 30 minutes.

149 Calories
3.0 g Protein
19.6 g Carbohydrates
7.7 g Fat
46.5% Calories from Fat
3.3 g Fiber
125 mg Sodium
0 mg Cholesterol

WHEN READY TO GRILL

Over hot coals, place the red peppers on a grill coated with vegetable spray. Cover grill and cook 14 to 20 minutes, or until skins are charred all over, turning peppers as skins blacken. Place the peppers in a plastic bag for 15 minutes. When peppers are cool enough to handle, peel away the skin and remove the top and seeds (do not rinse the peppers). Cut peppers into strips and set aside.

Pour 1 tablespoon olive oil into a plastic bag. Add eggplant slices and zucchini and turn to coat all over. Remove vegetables to a plate. Add 1 tablespoon olive oil to same bag and add onions; turn to coat.

Thread onions on skewers. Place eggplant slices, zucchini, and onions on grill. Cover grill and cook eggplant and zucchini 4 to 5 minutes on each side, or until brown and tender; cook onions for 10 to 12 minutes, turning onions every 4 minutes. Allow vegetables to cool for 10 minutes. Cut the eggplant into cubes and the zucchini and onions into $\frac{1}{4}$ inch thick slices.

Preheat oven to 350°.

Coat a small pan with nonstick vegetable spray and place over moderate heat. Add garlic and cook 2 to 3 minutes, stirring frequently. Combine garlic, red pepper, eggplant, and onions in an $8 \times 11.5 \times 2$-inch oblong baking dish that has been coated with a nonstick vegetable spray and spread it evenly. Place an overlapping row of tomatoes over vegetables, starting at one short end of dish. Overlap a row of zucchini slices against tomatoes and continue this process with the remaining zucchini and tomato slices. Sprinkle the vegetables with thyme, savory, salt, and pepper and drizzle 1 tablespoon olive oil over all. Bake for 30 minutes. Remove eggplant au gratin from oven and top with bread crumbs and drizzle the last 1 tablespoon olive oil on top. Bake 15 minutes.

4 SERVINGS

I like to serve this hearty soup in the fall when it is still comfortable enough outside to grill outdoors yet the slight chill in the air makes this warm, spicy soup taste so good. Serve as the first course followed by grilled lamb and Saffron Rice (page 224).

1 eggplant (1 pound), sliced ½ inch thick
1 tablespoon extra-virgin olive oil
1 cup chopped onions
2 bay leaves
1 tablespoon minced garlic
1 teaspoon *each* thyme and basil
½ teaspoon freshly ground pepper
¼ teaspoon salt
1 can (28 ounces) crushed tomatoes with
   tomato puree
1 cup fatfree chicken broth

Place eggplant in a colander and sprinkle with salt. Allow the eggplant to sit for 30 minutes.

WHEN READY TO GRILL
Over hot coals, place eggplant on a grill coated with nonstick vegetable spray. Cover grill and cook 5 to 6 minutes on each side, or until eggplant is brown and soft. Remove skin and cut eggplant into cubes.

Coat a large saucepan with nonstick vegetable spray and add olive oil. Place saucepan over moderate heat for 1 minute. Add onions, bay leaves, garlic, thyme, basil, pepper, and salt and cook 5 minutes, stirring occasionally. Add eggplant, tomatoes, and chicken broth, cover, and cook 10 minutes. Remove bay leaves before serving.

126 Calories
4.0 g Protein
20.6 g Carbohydrates
4.0 g Fat
28.9% Calories from Fat
2.6 g Fiber
909 mg Sodium
0 mg Cholesterol

4 SERVINGS

Belgian endive leaves are 5 to 6 inches long and are tightly wrapped, resembling a cigar. Grilling this exotic leaf allows it to be served as a vegetable side dish rather than its more traditional use as a salad ingredient.

4 endives
8 teaspoons extra-virgin olive oil

WHEN READY TO GRILL
Cut endives in half and brush each side with ½ teaspoon olive oil. Over hot coals, place endive on a grill coated with nonstick vegetable spray. Cover grill and cook 6 to 8 minutes on each side, or until tender.

89 Calories
0.5 g Protein
2.1 g Carbohydrates
9.1 g Fat
92.3% Calories from Fat
0.9 g Fiber
1 mg Sodium
0 mg Cholesterol

4 SERVINGS

*Florence fennel is a white bulbous root with heavy stalks
growing from the top that resemble celery. It has a wonderful anise
flavor and can be eaten both raw or cooked—grilling it is ideal!*

2 fennel
½ tablespoon extra-virgin olive oil

Trim the tops and remove the outer leaves and ends of
the fennel. Remove the ends, outer leaves, and trim the
tops of the fennel. Cut the fennel into quarters and
thread them onto skewers; brush with olive oil.

WHEN READY TO GRILL
Over hot coals, place fennel on a grill coated with nonstick
vegetable spray. Cover grill and cook 16 to 20 minutes, or
until brown and tender, turning every 3 minutes.

48 Calories
1.3 g Protein
7.6 g Carbohydrates
2.0 g Fat
37.1% Calories from Fat
1.7 g Fiber
54 mg Sodium
0 mg Cholesterol

4 SERVINGS

This fabulous recipe, featured in the Des Moines Register, *comes from Kingsford, a company known for a variety of charcoal briquettes and grilling accessories. Serve this salad with grilled lamb and warmed whole wheat pita pockets.*

¼ cup extra-virgin olive oil

1 tablespoon fresh lemon juice

2 teaspoons pressed garlic

1 teaspoon oregano

1 pound fresh vegetables (eggplant, assorted summer squash, bell peppers, mushrooms, and onions)

Combine olive oil, lemon juice, garlic, and oregano; set aside.

Slice eggplant into half-inch rounds. Cut small squash in half lengthwise; cut larger squash into ½-inch pieces. Cut bell peppers into large chunks. Cut onions into wedges or rounds. Toss vegetables with garlic oil to coat.

WHEN READY TO GRILL

Place vegetables in a single layer on grilling rack in covered grill over medium-hot coals. Grill 10 to 20 minutes, or until tender, turning once and basting with any remaining garlic oil. Remove vegetables as they become done and keep warm.

155 Calories
1.6 g Protein
7.9 g Carbohydrates
13.8 g Fat
80.3% Calories from Fat
1.6 g Fiber
3 mg Sodium
0 mg Cholesterol

4 SERVINGS

The Japanese eggplant has a rich purple color and is long and slender. It is available in most Asian food stores.

3 to 4 Japanese eggplants, cut in half
3 to 4 teaspoons Fiery Hot Pepper Oil (page 226)

WHEN READY TO GRILL
Brush each side of eggplant with ½ teaspoon Fiery Hot Pepper Oil. Over hot coals, place eggplant slices on a grill coated with nonstick vegetable spray. Cover grill and cook eggplant for about 5 minutes on each side, or until golden brown.

54 Calories
0.6 g Protein
3.5 g Carbohydrates
4.5 g Fat
74.7% Calories from Fat
0.6 g Fiber
1 mg Sodium
0 mg Cholesterol

4 SERVINGS

The potatoes acquire a smoky flavor from the grill. Serve topped
with lowfat sour cream and Gazpacho Salsa (page 90).

4 baking potatoes
4 teaspoons extra-virgin olive oil

WHEN READY TO GRILL
Prick potatoes all over with a fork and rub the skin of each
one with 1 teaspoon olive oil. Over hot coals, place potatoes on a grill. Cover grill and cook 30 to 35 minutes, or
until potatoes feel soft when lightly squeezed, turning
potatoes occasionally.

220 Calories
4.7 g Protein
51.0 g Carbohydrates
0.2 g Fat
0.8% Calories from Fat
2.4 g Fiber
16 mg Sodium
0 mg Cholesterol

8 SERVINGS

*This is a fabulous salad that combines the smoky flavor
of roasted red pepper, yellow squash, and Bermuda onions with a
Greek Salad Dressing and pasta. It can be served as the main course with
chunks of crusty French bread or try it as a side dish with grilled chicken.*

Greek Salad Dressing
1 clove garlic
2 tablespoons *each* fresh lemon juice and
   red wine vinegar
1 tablespoon oregano
½ teaspoon freshly ground pepper
5 tablespoons extra-virgin olive oil

Pasta
1 red pepper
1 crookneck squash, halved
1 tablespoon extra-virgin olive oil
1 Bermuda onion, peeled and quartered
12 ounces rigatoni
6 ounces fresh spinach, washed, dried, and torn
   into bite-size pieces
6 ounces feta cheese, crumbled
½ cup Greek olives, pitted and sliced

331 Calories
9.4 g Protein
35.9 g Carbohydrates
17.2 g Fat
46.7% Calories from Fat
4.1 g Fiber
388 mg Sodium
19 mg Cholesterol

To make Greek Salad Dressing

In work bowl of food processor fitted with a metal blade, process garlic until chopped. Add lemon juice, red wine vinegar, oregano, and pepper and process until combined. Add olive oil in a slow steady stream and process until well blended. Set aside.

WHEN READY TO GRILL

Over hot coals, place the red pepper on a grill coated with nonstick vegetable spray. Cover grill and cook 14 to 20 minutes or until skin is charred all over, turning pepper as skin blackens. Place pepper in a plastic bag for 15 minutes. When the pepper is cool enough to handle, peel away the skin and remove the top and the seeds (do not rinse the pepper). Cut pepper into thin strips and set aside.

Place summer squash on grill and brush with olive oil. Cover grill and cook 3 to 4 minutes on each side. Cut into thin slices. Set aside.

Thread Bermuda onion on a skewer and brush with olive oil. Place onion on grill and cook, covered, 10 to 12 minutes, turning every 3 minutes. Slice onion into slivers. Set aside.

Cook rigatoni according to package instructions. Drain well.

In a large bowl, combine rigatoni, red pepper, squash, onion, spinach, feta cheese, and olives and toss to blend. Add dressing and blend well. Serve at room temperature or refrigerate, covered, for several hours or overnight.

4 (1-CUP) SERVINGS

*This is a spicy soup that marvelously combines the contrasting
flavors of roasted corn, jalapeño peppers, and spicy hot croutons.
Serve as the first course, followed by grilled seafood and a fresh fruit salad.*

Spicy Croutons

1½ cups firm-textured, fatfree bread, cut into
    ½-inch cubes
2 tablespoons extra-virgin olive oil
½ teaspoon *each* cumin and thyme
⅛ teaspoon *each* cayenne and freshly
    ground pepper

Mexican Corn Soup

6 ears of fresh corn
¼ cup (½ stick) light margarine
2 tablespoons minced onions
3 jalapeños, seeded and minced*
1 cup water
2 cups skimmed evaporated milk
½ teaspoon hot pepper sauce
¼ teaspoon *each* salt and freshly ground pepper

½ cup lowfat cheddar cheese

*The seeds of jalapeño peppers are very hot. To avoid burning your skin, wear rubber or latex gloves when removing the seeds. Immediately wash the knife, cutting surface, and gloves when finished.

469 Calories
23.5 g Protein
55.4 g Carbohydrates
19.7 g Fat
37.9% Calories from Fat
5.4 g Fiber
733 mg Sodium
25 mg Cholesterol

To make spicy croutons

Preheat oven to 350°.

Place bread cubes on a baking sheet and bake 12 to 14 minutes, or until lightly browned.

Place a large saucepan over moderate heat and add olive oil. Add toasted bread cubes, cumin, thyme, cayenne, and pepper and blend well. Cook 1 to 2 minutes, or until heated through. Set aside. (Can be made a day ahead and stored in an airtight container.)

To make Mexican Corn Soup

Gently peel back, but do not detach, the layers of husk on each corn, and remove the exposed fine threads. Remove one of the outer pieces of husk to use as a string and set aside. Gently return the remaining husk to its original shape around the corn, twisting it at the top. Secure the twisted top by tying the reserved husk around it. Soak the corn in cold water for 30 minutes; drain.

WHEN READY TO GRILL

Over hot coals, place the corn on a grill. Cover grill and cook 25 to 30 minutes, turning corn occasionally.

Remove the browned husks from the corn. Using a corn husker or sharp knife, remove the kernels from the corn.

In a large saucepan over moderate heat, melt margarine. Add corn kernels, onion, and jalapeños and cook 5 minutes, stirring occasionally. Remove mixture to work bowl of food processor fitted with a metal blade and process until pureed. Transfer mixture pack to saucepan and add water, evaporated milk, hot pepper sauce, salt, and pepper and cook 3 to 5 minutes, or until heated through.

WHEN READY TO SERVE

Divide the soup among four soup bowls and garnish each serving with 2 tablespoons of cheese and some Spicy Croutons.

8 SERVINGS

The flavors of the grilled vegetables mingle perfectly with the herbs and spices as they bake together. Ratatouille can be a delicious appetizer spooned onto toast points, a side dish, even as a complete meal when served on a bed of steamed brown rice.

1 eggplant (1 pound), cut into ½-inch slices
3 tablespoons extra-virgin olive oil
1 zucchini, halved
1 crookneck squash, halved
1 onion, quartered
2 cloves garlic, minced
¼ cup chopped parsley
1 can (28 ounces) crushed tomatoes with
   tomato puree
1 teaspoon *each* basil and oregano
¼ teaspoon *each* salt and freshly ground pepper
¼ cup chopped fresh basil

Sprinkle salt over eggplant and place in a colander for 30 minutes.

Pour 2 tablespoons of the olive oil into a plastic bag. Add eggplant, zucchini, and squash and toss to coat all over. Remove vegetables to a plate. Add onions to the same bag and toss to coat. Place the onions on skewers.

103 Calories
2.3 g Protein
12.8 g Carbohydrates
5.6 g Fat
48.5% Calories from Fat
2.2 g Fiber
332 mg Sodium
0 mg Cholesterol

WHEN READY TO GRILL

Over hot coals place the vegetables on a grill coated with nonstick vegetable spray. Cover grill and cook eggplant, zucchini, and squash 4 to 5 minutes on each side and the onions for 10 to 12 minutes, turning onions every 4 minutes.

When vegetables are cool enough to handle, cut the eggplant into cubes and the zucchini, squash, and onion into slices.

In a large saucepan over moderate heat, cook the garlic in 1 tablespoon olive oil for 2 minutes. Add the eggplant, zucchini, squash, onions, parsley, tomatoes, 1 teaspoon dried basil, oregano, salt, and pepper and blend well. Cover saucepan and cook over moderately low heat for 30 minutes. Add ¼ cup fresh basil and blend well.

4 SERVINGS

Grilled Sweet Potatoes make a delicious accompaniment to turkey or other poultry.

4 sweet potatoes
4 teaspoons extra-virgin olive oil

WHEN READY TO GRILL
Prick sweet potatoes all over with a fork. Rub 1 teaspoon olive oil over each sweet potato. Over hot coals, place the potatoes on grill. Cover grill and cook 1 hour, or until potatoes are soft when lightly squeezed, turning occasionally.

118 Calories
2.0 g Protein
27.7 g Carbohydrates
0.1 g Fat
1.0% Calories from Fat
3.4 g Fiber
12 mg Sodium
0 mg Cholesterol

4 SERVINGS

*This colorful array of grilled vegetables will complement any meal.
It is also the perfect main-dish meal for vegetarian lovers! Serve with
chunks of feta cheese or other lowfat cheese and a loaf of French bread.*

Marinade

¼ cup balsamic vinegar
1 tablespoon sherry vinegar
⅛ teaspoon *each* salt and freshly ground pepper
1 clove garlic, minced

1 Japanese eggplant, sliced ¼ inch thick
1 *each* red, yellow, and orange pepper, seeded,
    each cut into 4 pieces
1 zucchini, halved
1 Bermuda onion, cut into 8 wedges

To make marinade

In a small heavy saucepan over moderately high heat,
bring balsamic vinegar to a boil. Continue boiling 7 to 8
minutes, or until vinegar is reduced to 2 tablespoons.
Cool to room temperature. Add sherry vinegar, salt,
pepper, and garlic and blend well. Place vegetables in a
nonmetal dish and pour marinade over top. Toss vegetables to coat all over. Cover dish and refrigerate 1 to
2 hours.

WHEN READY TO GRILL

Over hot coals, place a grilling wok coated with nonstick
vegetable spray on a grill. Add vegetables and stir-fry
1 minute. Cover grill and cook 2 minutes. Repeat process
2 more times or until vegetables are tender and golden
brown.

66 Calories
1.8 g Protein
15.4 g Carbohydrates
0.3 g Fat
4.0% Calories from Fat
2.8 g Fiber
72 mg Sodium
0 mg Cholesterol

4 SERVINGS

Roasting the tomatoes on a grill imparts a new dimension to the taste of this ever-popular summer soup. It can be enjoyed warm or chilled. Serve with grilled chicken.

4 large tomatoes, sliced ½ inch thick

2 tablespoons extra-virgin olive oil

1 medium onion, sliced

1 medium carrot, coarsely chopped

1 stalk celery, coarsely chopped

2 tablespoons parsley, chopped

2 tablespoons minced fresh basil

1 bay leaf

1 teaspoon *each* thyme and freshly
    ground pepper

½ teaspoon salt

3 tablespoons tomato paste

1 tablespoon flour

1 can (14½ ounces) fatfree chicken broth

½ cup skimmed evaporated milk

168 Calories
6.2 g Protein
21.2 g Carbohydrates
7.6 g Fat
40.6% Calories from Fat
3.9 g Fiber
880 mg Sodium
1 mg Cholesterol

WHEN READY TO GRILL

Over hot coals, place tomato slices on a grill coated with nonstick vegetable spray. Cover grill and cook tomatoes for 4 minutes on each side, or until nicely browned.

Place olive oil in a large saucepan over moderately low heat. Add onion, carrot, celery, parsley, basil, bay leaf, thyme, pepper, and salt and cook 5 minutes. Add grilled tomatoes and tomato paste and cook 5 to 6 minutes. Add flour and blend well. Add chicken broth and simmer 20 minutes, covered.

Remove saucepan from heat and discard bay leaf. Allow the soup to sit for 10 minutes. Transfer mixture to work bowl of food processor fitted with a metal blade and process until pureed. Return pureed mixture to saucepan; add evaporated milk and blend well. Cook soup 3 to 5 minutes, or until heated through. Taste for seasoning.

If serving the soup hot, serve immediately and garnish each serving with chopped chives or parsley. If serving the soup chilled, refrigerate, covered, for several hours or overnight.

4 SERVINGS

The vegetables can be lightly brushed with olive oil before grilling; however, I prefer to make them with this flavorful marinade. Cold leftovers are delicious mixed with a little feta cheese and stuffed in pitas or tossed with warm pasta.

WHEN READY TO GRILL

Alternate squash, mushrooms, red pepper, onions, and eggplant onto skewers (reserving marinade). Over hot coals, place the vegetables on a grill coated with nonstick vegetable spray. Cover grill and cook 10 to 15 minutes, or until the vegetables are brown and tender, turning the skewers every 3 minutes and brushing with reserved marinade.

136 Calories
1.9 g Protein
9.5 g Carbohydrates
10.9 g Fat
72.2% Calories from Fat
1.7 g Fiber
103 mg Sodium
0 mg Cholesterol

Marinade

3 tablespoons extra-virgin olive oil
2 tablespoons *each* red wine vinegar and fresh lemon juice
1 tablespoon Dijon mustard
1 tablespoon *each* chopped fresh basil and parsley
1 large clove garlic, minced
$\frac{1}{8}$ teaspoon freshly ground pepper

Kebab Vegetables

1 small yellow squash, sliced $\frac{1}{4}$ inch thick
4 mushroom caps
1 red pepper, cut into 8 pieces
1 Bermuda onion, cut into chunks
1 Japanese eggplant, sliced $\frac{1}{4}$ inch thick

To make marinade

Combine olive oil, red wine vinegar, lemon juice, mustard, basil, parsley, garlic, and pepper in a 1-gallon reclosable plastic bag. Add squash, mushrooms, red pepper, onion, and eggplant and toss to coat vegetables. Refrigerate 2 to 3 hours.

4 SERVINGS

Yams are perfect for grilling. They are sweeter and larger than sweet potatoes and their skin is usually purplish or reddish brown in color rather than orange.

1½ tablespoons extra-virgin olive oil
4 yams, sliced ½ inch thick

WHEN READY TO GRILL
Pour olive oil into a plastic bag and add yams; turn to coat all over. Over hot coals, place yams on a grill coated with nonstick vegetable spray. Cover grill and cook 10 minutes on each side, or until brown and tender.

203 Calories
2.0 g Protein
37.5 g Carbohydrates
5.3 g Fat
23.5% Calories from Fat
4.1 g Fiber
11 mg Sodium
0 mg Cholesterol

4 SERVINGS

This wonderful salad is similar to antipasto. It can be
served as the first course or as a salad after the meal.

Balsamic Vinaigrette

1 shallot

2 tablespoons balsamic vinegar

2 teaspoons Dijon mustard

$\frac{1}{8}$ teaspoon *each* salt and freshly ground pepper

5 tablespoons extra-virgin olive oil

2 large red peppers

1 eggplant, cut into $\frac{1}{4}$-inch slices

$1\frac{1}{2}$ tablespoons extra-virgin olive oil

1 zucchini, sliced diagonally into $\frac{1}{4}$-inch slices

1 crookneck squash, sliced diagonally into
    $\frac{1}{4}$-inch slices

Part-skimmed milk mozzarella cheese (8 ounces),
    cut into wedges

8 black olives, pitted

400 Calories
15.9 g Protein
13.2 g Carbohydrates
32.6 g Fat
73.3% Calories from Fat
2.2 g Fiber
480 mg Sodium
32 mg Cholesterol

To make Balsamic Vinaigrette

In work bowl of food processor fitted with a metal blade, process shallot until chopped. Add balsamic vinegar, mustard, salt, and pepper and process until blended. Add 5 tablespoons of the olive oil in a slow steady stream and process until well blended. Pour vinaigrette into a cruet and set aside.

Place eggplant slices in a colander and sprinkle with salt. Allow eggplant to sit for 30 minutes.

WHEN READY TO GRILL

Over hot coals, place the red peppers on a grill coated with nonstick vegetable spray and cook 14 to 20 minutes, or until skins are charred all over, turning peppers as skins blacken. Place peppers in a plastic bag for 15 minutes. When peppers are cool enough to handle, peel away the skin and remove the top and seeds (do not rinse the peppers). Cut the peppers into quarters and set aside.

Place eggplant in a plastic bag and add ½ tablespoon olive oil; turn to coat all over. Place eggplant on grill and cook 4 minutes on each side, or until tender. Set aside.

Place zucchini and yellow squash slices in a bag and add 1 tablespoon olive oil; turn to coat all over. Place slices on a grilling grid coated with nonstick vegetable spray and cook 3 to 4 minutes on each side, or until tender.

WHEN READY TO SERVE

Arrange vegetables on a platter with slices of mozzarella cheese and olives and serve with Balsamic Vinaigrette. Allow guests or family members to prepare their own salads.

4 SERVINGS

*This pizza is definitely a favorite among my children and their friends.
The naan (Indian bread) is the perfect size for making individual size pizzas
and it makes a wonderful crispy crust when cooked on the grill and topped
with the cheese and vegetables. Naan is available in most Asian food stores.*

4 teaspoons extra-virgin olive oil

4 naan breads

1½ cups skimmed milk mozzarella cheese

4 teaspoons minced garlic

1 large yellow pepper, seeded and thinly sliced

1 large tomato, thinly sliced

1 small bunch broccoli florets, parboiled 1 minute
  and thinly sliced*

1½ cups skimmed milk mozzarella cheese

*This pizza can be made with any of your favorite vegetables.

443 Calories
28.2 g Protein
34.2 g Carbohydrates
22.3 g Fat
45.2% Calories from Fat
3.4 g Fiber
439 mg Sodium
48 mg Cholesterol

Brush 1 teaspoon oil on a naan and sprinkle 6 table-spoons cheese, 1 teaspoon garlic, and one fourth of the red pepper, tomato, and broccoli slices all over; top with 6 tablespoons cheese. Repeat this process with the remaining naan.

WHEN READY TO GRILL

Prepare grill with charcoal on only one half of the grill and place an aluminum pan on the empty side. When coals are hot, place a prepared pizza over coals on a grill coated with nonstick vegetable spray. Cover grill and cook 1 minute. Using a very wide spatula or tongs, move pizza directly over the aluminum pan and away from the coals. Cover grill and cook 10 minutes, or until cheese has melted and vegetables are heated through. Prepare remaining 3 pizzas in the same way.

8 SERVINGS

*These veggie burgers are chock-full of wholesome vegetables
and grains. They are wonderful topped with lettuce, thinly sliced
Vidalia onions, tomatoes, green pepper, and alfalfa sprouts and nestled in
whole–wheat buns. Serve with mugs of Roasted Red Pepper Soup (page 280).*

½ cup bulgur
¾ cup boiling water
½ cup water
¼ cup quinoa
4 shallots
1 can (19 ounces) cannelloni beans, drained
1 cup bread crumbs
¾ cup packed chopped fresh spinach
½ cup chopped carrots
¼ cup packed chopped parsley
2 tablespoons *each* chopped celery and walnuts
2 mushrooms, chopped
½ tablespoon Worcestershire sauce
½ teaspoon freshly ground pepper

164 Calories
7.2 g Protein
31.1 g Carbohydrates
1.7 g Fat
9.2% Calories from Fat
4.3 g Fiber
279 mg Sodium
1 mg Cholesterol

Place bulgur in a large mixing bowl and pour ¾ cup boiling water over it. Let sit for 15 minutes. Transfer bulgur to a sieve and drain well. Push down on the bulgur with a spoon to remove as much water as possible. Return bulgur to mixing bowl and set aside.

In a small saucepan, bring ½ cup water to a boil over moderately high heat. Add quinoa, reduce heat, cover, and cook 20 minutes. Add quinoa to bulgur.

In work bowl of food processor fitted with a metal blade, process shallots until finely chopped. Add cannelloni beans and puree. Add bread crumbs, spinach, carrots, parsley, celery, walnuts, mushrooms, Worcestershire sauce, and pepper and blend well. Form the mixture into 8 veggie burgers.

Over hot coals, place burgers on grill coated with nonstick vegetable spray. Cover grill and cook 8 to 12 minutes, turning burgers every 3 minutes.

4 SERVINGS

This is a delightful way to serve zucchini and yellow squash.
The ribbon shapes and colorful vegetables add a festive touch to any meal.

1 pound zucchini
1 pound yellow squash
2 tablespoons extra-virgin olive oil
1 tablespoon fresh lemon juice
2 cloves garlic, minced
1 tablespoon sherry vinegar
¼ teaspoon *each* salt and freshly ground pepper

Cut the zucchini and yellow squash into ribbons 4 inches long, ¾ inch wide, and ¼ inch thick (the measurement does not have to be exact). Place the ribbons in a plastic bag containing olive oil, lemon juice, and garlic and turn to coat all over.

WHEN READY TO GRILL
Over hot coals, place zucchini and yellow squash ribbons in a grilling wok coated with nonstick vegetable spray. Cover grill and cook 12 minutes, turning vegetables every 3 minutes. Transfer vegetables to a serving bowl and toss with sherry vinegar, salt, and pepper.

102 Calories
2.8 g Protein
9.3 g Carbohydrates
7.2 g Fat
63.5% Calories from Fat
2.6 g Fiber
140 mg Sodium
0 mg Cholesterol

6 SERVINGS

*The smoky flavor of grilled zucchini harmonizes beautifully
with the onions and seasonings. Serve soup either warm or chilled
along with Pitas with Grilled Vegetables and Tahini Sauce.*

1 zucchini (1 pound), cut in half
1 large onion, thinly sliced
3 cups fatfree chicken broth
1 teaspoon dried basil
½ teaspoon salt
¼ teaspoon freshly ground white pepper
½ cup skimmed evaporated milk
Chopped chives or parsley

WHEN READY TO GRILL

Over hot coals, place zucchini on a grill coated with non-stick vegetable spray. Cover grill and cook zucchini for 3 to 4 minutes on each side.

Slice zucchini into 1-inch chunks and place in a medium saucepan over moderate heat. Add onion, chicken broth, basil, salt, and pepper and bring to a boil. Reduce heat, cover, and simmer 10 minutes.

Depending on the size of your work bowl, transfer all or half of the soup to work bowl of food processor fitted with a metal blade and process until pureed. Return soup to saucepan and add skimmed milk. Cook until heated through. Garnish each serving with chopped chives or parsley.

47 Calories
3.9 g Protein
8.2 g Carbohydrates
0.2 g Fat
4.3% Calories from Fat
1.4 g Fiber
698 mg Sodium
1 mg Cholesterol

4 SERVINGS

*Portobello mushrooms are giant, cultivated mushrooms that
are dark brown in color and have an open cap. They are delicious
combined with garlicky sauce and pasta. Serve with crusty bread.*

Garlic Sauce

1 cup loosely packed parsley
2 green onions, cut into 2-inch pieces
3 cloves garlic
1 tablespoon white wine vinegar
1 teaspoon thyme
¼ teaspoon *each* salt and freshly ground pepper
¼ cup extra-virgin olive oil

1 red pepper
1 package ziti (16 ounces)
10 ounces Portobello mushrooms, sliced
   ½ inch thick
1 tablespoon extra-virgin olive oil
1½ tablespoons parmesan cheese

587 Calories
16.5 g Protein
86.4 g Carbohydrates
19.8 g Fat
30.4% Calories from Fat
9.6 g Fiber
183 mg Sodium
2 mg Cholesterol

To make Garlic Sauce

In work bowl of food processor fitted with metal blade, process parsley, green onions, and garlic until finely chopped. Add white wine vinegar, thyme, salt, and pepper and process until blended. Add olive oil in a slow steady stream and process until well blended. Set aside.

WHEN READY TO GRILL

Over hot coals, place the red pepper on a grill. Cover grill and cook pepper 14 to 20 minutes, or until skin is charred all over, turning pepper as skin blackens. Place pepper in a plastic bag for 15 minutes. When pepper is cool enough to handle, peel away the skin and remove the top and seeds (do not rinse the pepper). Cut the pepper into strips and set aside.

Cook ziti according to package directions, drain, and keep warm.

While ziti is cooking, place mushroom slices on skewers and brush with olive oil. Over hot coals, place mushrooms on a grill coated with nonstick vegetable spray. Cover grill and cook mushrooms 5 minutes on each side. Cut mushrooms into thin slices.

Place ziti, pepper, mushrooms, and parmesan cheese in a large serving bowl. Pour Garlic Sauce over pasta mixture and blend well.

4 SERVINGS

Tahini is made of toasted and hulled sesame seeds that are
ground into a paste and is frequently used in Middle Eastern cooking.
It is fabulous in combination with lemon juice, spices, and yogurt and it
highlights the smoky flavor of grilled vegetables. Serve with Tabbouleh.

Grilled Vegetables

1 eggplant (12 ounces), peeled and diced
1 yellow pepper
1½ tablespoons extra-virgin olive oil
4 plum tomatoes, chopped
2 cloves garlic
⅛ teaspoon *each* salt and freshly ground pepper
2 tablespoons chopped parsley
4 pita breads, halved and warmed according to package directions

Tahini Sauce

2 cloves garlic
½ cup coarsely chopped parsley
6 tablespoons plain nonfat yogurt
¼ cup fresh lemon juice
3 tablespoons tahini
2 tablespoons cumin
⅛ teaspoon *each* salt and freshly ground white pepper

Tabbouleh

1 cup bulgur
1½ cups water
1 teaspoon salt
¼ cup fresh lemon juice
1 teaspoon minced garlic
¼ cup extra-virgin olive oil
½ teaspoon dried mint
¼ teaspoon freshly ground pepper
1 cup packed chopped parsley
½ cup chopped green onions
2 tomatoes, chopped

To make Tahini Sauce

In work bowl of food processor fitted with a metal blade, process garlic and parsley until finely chopped. Add yogurt, lemon juice, tahini, cumin, salt, and white pepper and process until blended. Refrigerate sauce in a covered container until ready to serve.

To make Tabbouleh

Combine bulgur, boiling water, and salt in a medium bowl and allow to sit, covered, for 20 minutes. Drain and push down on the bulgur with a spoon to remove as much water as possible. Add lemon juice, garlic, olive oil, mint, and pepper and blend well. Refrigerate, covered for 3 hours. When ready to serve, add parsley, green onions, and chopped tomatoes and blend well. Makes 3 cups.

To make Grilled Vegetables

Place eggplant in a colander and sprinkle lightly with salt. Let sit 30 minutes.

WHEN READY TO GRILL

Over hot coals, place the yellow pepper on a grill. Cover grill and cook 14 to 20 minutes or until skin is charred all over, turning pepper as skin blackens. Place pepper in a plastic bag for 15 minutes. When the pepper is cool enough to handle, peel away the skin and remove the top and seeds (do not rinse the pepper). Cut the pepper into thin slices and set aside.

Pour $1\frac{1}{2}$ tablespoons olive oil into a plastic bag and add eggplant, chopped plum tomatoes, and garlic; turn to coat all over. Place mixture in a grilling wok coated with non-stick vegetable spray on grill. Cover grill and cook 10 minutes, turning frequently. Transfer vegetable mixture to a small bowl. Add pepper slices, salt, pepper, and parsley to eggplant mixture in small bowl and blend well.

WHEN READY TO SERVE

Fill warmed pita halves two thirds full with vegetable filling. Top with 1 tablespoon Tahini Sauce.

340 Calories
17.2 g Protein
48.0 g Carbohydrates
9.9 g Fat
26.2% Calories from Fat
3.9 g Fiber
467 mg Sodium
3 mg Cholesterol

4 SERVINGS

The contrast of the yellow pepper and the red tomato makes an eye-appealing salad that complements any meal, especially Middle Eastern entrees.

Dressing
2 tablespoons parsley
1 clove garlic
1 tablespoon *each* fresh lemon juice and
   white wine vinegar
¼ teaspoon *each* cumin, salt, and sugar

⅛ teaspoon *each* paprika, cayenne, and pepper
3 tablespoons extra-virgin olive oil

3 yellow peppers
2 large tomatoes, seeded and cut into thin strips
Chopped parsley
8 kalamata olives

159 Calories
2.2 g Protein
13.4 g Carbohydrates
12.1 g Fat
68.6% Calories from Fat
3.2 g Fiber
270 mg Sodium
0 mg Cholesterol

To make Dressing

In work bowl of food processor, process parsley and garlic until finely chopped. Add lemon juice, white wine vinegar, cumin, salt, sugar, paprika, cayenne, and pepper and process until smooth. Add olive oil in a slow steady stream and process until well blended. Set aside (do not refrigerate the dressing).

WHEN READY TO GRILL

Over hot coals, place the yellow peppers on a grill. Cover grill and cook 14 to 20 minutes, or until skins are charred all over, turning peppers as skins blacken. Place the peppers in a plastic bag for 15 minutes. When peppers are cool enough to handle, peel away the skin and remove the top and seeds (do not rinse the pepper). Cut peppers into $\frac{1}{8}$-inch strips and place in a medium bowl. Add the sliced tomatoes and enough dressing to coat and gently mix.

WHEN READY TO SERVE

Place a large piece of curly leaf lettuce on individual salad plates and divide the peppers and tomatoes among them. Garnish each serving with 2 olives and parsley, if desired.

4 SERVINGS

This soup is for roasted red pepper lovers! The exacting balance
of the peppers' rich aroma and savory flavor permeates the broth. It can
be enjoyed as a hot soup and is equally delicious served at room
temperature. Serve with crostini and a salad of mixed baby greens.

4 large red peppers
2 leeks, cut into 1-inch pieces
$\frac{1}{4}$ cup light margarine
6 cloves garlic, minced
2 cans (10$\frac{1}{2}$ ounces each) fatfree chicken broth
$\frac{1}{2}$ teaspoon *each* salt and freshly ground pepper
$\frac{1}{2}$ cup skimmed evaporated milk
Chopped fresh chives

WHEN READY TO GRILL
Over hot coals, place the peppers on a grill. Cover grill and cook 14 to 20 minutes, or until skins are charred all over, turning peppers as skins blacken. Place peppers in a plastic bag for 15 minutes. When the peppers are cool enough to handle, peel away the skin and remove the top and seeds (do not rinse the pepper).

Place leeks in a bowl of cold water to remove any grit. Drain and coarsely chop.

Melt margarine in a large saucepan over moderate heat. Add leeks and garlic and cook over low heat, covered, for 5 minutes. Add red peppers, chicken broth, salt, and pepper and cook over moderate heat for 15 minutes. Transfer mixture to a work bowl of a food processor fitted with a metal blade and process until pureed. Add evaporated milk and blend well. Garnish each serving with chopped chives.

113 Calories
4.8 g Protein
11.3 g Carbohydrates
5.9 g Fat
47.4% Calories from Fat
1.3 g Fiber
1093 mg Sodium
1 mg Cholesterol

¾ CUP

On a recent trip to San Francisco, I ventured into a farmer's market laden with fabulous fruits, vegetables, flowers, and wonderful gourmet foods to taste. My favorite item was an eggplant pesto. To reduce the fat, I cut down on the amount of olive oil. This gave my pesto a thicker consistency—but the taste remains sensational!

2 tablespoons extra-virgin olive oil
3 Japanese eggplants (5 to 6 ounces each), sliced
 ½ inch thick
1 cup loosely packed parsley
3 cloves garlic
1½ tablespoons tahini (optional)*
¼ teaspoon *each* salt and freshly ground pepper

Soak 1 cup of your favorite smoking wood chips in water for 30 minutes.

WHEN READY TO GRILL
Pour 1 tablespoon of the olive oil into a plastic bag and add eggplant; turn to coat all over. Sprinkle wet smoking chips over hot coals. Place eggplant slices on a grilling grid coated with nonstick vegetable spray. Cover grill and cook 5 minutes on each side, or until eggplant is golden brown. Allow eggplants to come to room temperature before removing skins.

In work bowl of food processor fitted with metal blade, process parsley and garlic until finely chopped. Add eggplant and process until smooth. Add optional tahini, remaining olive oil, salt, and pepper and process until well blended. Place eggplant pesto in a covered container and refrigerate for up to 1 week.

*Tahini is made of ground sesame seeds. It is available in most health food stores.

104 Calories
1.3 g Protein
5.2 g Carbohydrates
9.3 g Fat
80.2% Calories from Fat
1.3 g Fiber
190 mg Sodium
0 mg Cholesterol

MAKES 2 CUPS

When I was very young, my mother made a dish similar to this called "poor man's caviar." She baked the eggplant in the oven; however, I prefer to make it on the grill so the eggplant picks up a smoky flavor. Serve with cut-up pita bread or crackers.

1 eggplant (1 pound)
1 tablespoon toasted sesame seeds
6 green onions
3 tablespoons minced parsley
3 cloves garlic, minced
3 tablespoons fresh lemon juice
¼ cup tahini*
1 tablespoon *each* soy sauce and honey
1 tablespoon extra-virgin olive oil
⅛ teaspoon salt

*Tahini is made from ground, roasted sesame seeds and has the consistency of peanut butter. It is available in most health food stores.

48 Calories
1.2 g Protein
4.6 g Carbohydrates
3.1 g Fat
59.3% Calories from Fat
0.8 g Fiber
85 mg Sodium
0 mg Cholesterol

Cut eggplant into ¼-inch thick slices and lightly sprinkle both sides with salt. Place eggplant slices in a colander for 30 minutes.

Preheat oven to 350°.

Place sesame seeds in a small pan and bake 10 to 15 minutes, or until golden brown. Set aside.

WHEN READY TO GRILL
Over hot coals, place eggplant slices on a grill coated with nonstick vegetable spray. Cover grill and cook eggplant 5 to 6 minutes on both sides, or until brown and tender. Allow the eggplant to come to room temperature before removing skin. Set aside.

In work bowl of food processor fitted with a metal blade, process onions, parsley, and garlic until finely chopped. Add eggplant and process until blended. Add lemon juice, tahini, soy sauce, honey, sesame seeds, olive oil, and salt and process until smooth. Refrigerate spicy eggplant dip in a covered container for several hours or overnight.

4 SERVINGS

Tempeh (pronounced tem-pay*) is a vegetarian product
made from cooked, cultured soybeans. It can be baked, fried,
steamed, or broiled. Grilling tempeh reveals a new dimension of this
versatile lowfat food. Serve with brown rice and grilled Pineapple Rings.*

Marinade

½ cup pineapple juice
¼ cup rice vinegar
2 tablespoons soy sauce
1½ tablespoons honey
1 piece fresh ginger root, peeled and cut
    ½ inch thick

1 package (8 ounces) frozen tempeh, defrosted
    and cut into ¾-inch cubes
1 cup fresh pineapple chunks
2 carrots, thinly sliced and parboiled 3 minutes
1 green pepper, cut into ⅛ inch slices

198 Calories
11.8 g Protein
30.9 g Carbohydrates
4.6 g Fat
20.7% Calories from Fat
3.0 g Fiber
544 mg Sodium
0 mg Cholesterol

To make marinade

Combine pineapple juice, rice vinegar, soy sauce, honey, and ginger root in a nonmetal dish and blend well. Add tempeh and toss to coat pieces. Cover dish and refrigerate for several hours.

WHEN READY TO GRILL

Over hot coals, place a grilling wok coated with nonstick vegetable spray on a grill. Add tempeh (reserve marinade and discard ginger root) and stir-fry 1 minute. Cover grill and cook 2 minutes. Repeat process one more time.

While tempeh is cooking, add carrots and green pepper to marinade and blend well. Set aside.

Stir-fry tempeh for 1 minute, or until golden brown. Add carrots, green pepper, and pineapple, and stir-fry for 1 minute. Cover grill and cook 2 minutes, or until vegetables are heated through. Transfer stir-fry to serving dish and add marinade; blend well.

2 SERVINGS

*Tofu or bean curd is a soybean product that is very high in protein
and low in cholesterol. It is delicious combined with this marinade and vegetables
and grilled in a wok. Serve over a bed of steamed basmati brown rice.*

WHEN READY TO GRILL
Over hot coals, place tofu (reserve marinade, discarding ginger root) and vegetables in a wok coated with nonstick vegetable spray. Cover grill and cook 9 minutes, gently turning mixture every 3 minutes. Transfer mixture to a bowl. Pour marinade over tofu and blend well.

253 Calories
18.1 g Protein
31.1 g Carbohydrates
9.2 g Fat
32.9% Calories from Fat
4.7 g Fiber
2150 mg Sodium
0 mg Cholesterol

1 carton (10½ ounces) firm tofu

Marinade
¼ cup soy sauce
1 tablespoon *each* rice vinegar and honey
1 piece fresh ginger root
¼ teaspoon sesame oil

4 ounces bean sprouts
3 ounces shiitake mushrooms, washed and
  thinly sliced
1 carrot, cut into long, thin strips
3 ounces daikon radish, julienned
6 ounces bok choy, thinly sliced

Line a colander with a paper towel and place tofu on the paper. Cover tofu with another piece of paper towel and allow to sit 2 hours. Remove tofu from colander and cut into 1-inch cubes.

Combine soy sauce, rice vinegar, honey, ginger root, and sesame oil in a nonmetal dish and add tofu. Turn to coat pieces. Allow to sit 45 minutes.

4 SERVINGS

*This salad recipe is from a visiting professor at the University
of Iowa who insisted I include it in my cookbook. She learned how to make
it without a formal recipe when she lived in Turkey; consequently the
precise amounts of each ingredient were somewhat vague. I hope the recipe
I have derived from her description does this wonderful salad justice!*

1 pound Japanese eggplants, halved

1 tablespoon extra-virgin olive oil

1 clove garlic

1 tablespoon fresh lemon juice

¼ teaspoon freshly ground pepper

⅛ teaspoon salt

Chopped parsley

8 tomato wedges

8 kalamata olives

4 lemon wedges

2 pita pockets, quartered and warmed

WHEN READY TO GRILL

Brush eggplant halves with ½ tablespoon olive oil. Over hot coals, place eggplants on grill coated with nonstick vegetable spray. Cover grill and cook 5 minutes on each side. Cool to room temperature before removing skins.

In work bowl of food processor fitted with a metal blade, process garlic until chopped. Add eggplant and process until smooth. Add lemon juice, ½ tablespoon olive oil, pepper, and salt and process until just blended. The salad can be served at room temperature or refrigerated in a covered container for a few hours.

WHEN READY TO SERVE

Divide eggplant salad among four salad plates and garnish each serving with chopped parsley. Surround the salad with wedges of tomatoes and lemon, olives, and warm pita.

135 Calories
3.6 g Protein
20.0 g Carbohydrates
5.3 g Fat
35.0% Calories from Fat
1.8 g Fiber
306 mg Sodium
0 mg Cholesterol

FRUITS

4 SERVINGS

Choose firm apples so they retain their shape even over the heat of the grill.

4 apples, cored

WHEN READY TO GRILL
Cut apples into ½-inch slices and remove any seeds. Over hot coals, place apples on a grilling grid coated with non-stick vegetable spray. Cover grill and cook 4 to 5 minutes on each side, or until apples are golden brown and tender.

77 Calories
0.3 g Protein
20.0 g Carbohydrates
0.5 g Fat
5.8% Calories from Fat
2.9 g Fiber
1 mg Sodium
0 mg Cholesterol

4 SERVINGS

These bananas are delicious when served with grilled meats or poultry. They also become part of a delicious dessert served alongside of frozen fatfree yogurt.

4 bananas
3 tablespoons light margarine, melted

WHEN READY TO GRILL
Remove banana peel and cut bananas in half lengthwise. Brush each side with melted margarine. Over hot coals, place bananas on a grilling grid coated with nonstick vegetable spray. Cover grill and cook bananas 4 to 5 minutes on each side, or until golden brown.

143 Calories
1.2 g Protein
26.7 g Carbohydrates
4.8 g Fat
30.2% Calories from Fat
1.8 g Fiber
105 mg Sodium
0 mg Cholesterol

4 SERVINGS

Grilling the fresh fruit adds a wonderful smoky flavor that balances the sweetness of the fruit. These fruit kebabs make a delightful accompaniment to grilled chicken or pork or can be served as a dessert with a dish of fatfree frozen yogurt.

8 strawberries, hulled
2 bananas, cut into 8 chunks
2 kiwis, peeled and cut into 8 slices
8 (1-inch) cubes cantaloupe
8 (1-inch) cubes fresh pineapple

¼ cup pineapple juice

Soak 8 bamboo skewers in water for at least 30 minutes or overnight.

WHEN READY TO GRILL
Alternate strawberries, banana, kiwi, cantaloupe, and pineapple among the skewers. Brush the fruit with pineapple juice. Over medium-hot coals, place the skewers on a grill coated with nonstick vegetable spray. Cover grill and cook 6 to 8 minutes, turning skewers every 3 minutes and brushing with pineapple juice.

106 Calories
1.4 g Protein
26.5 g Carbohydrates
0.7 g Fat
5.9% Calories from Fat
3.1 g Fiber
5 mg Sodium
0 mg Cholesterol

4 SERVINGS

Like many grilled fruits, peaches make a wonderful
accompaniment to poultry or pork and can double as a dessert.

4 firm peaches, peeled, cut in half, pit removed

WHEN READY TO GRILL
Over medium-hot coals, place peaches on a grill coated
with nonstick vegetable spray. Cover grill and cook 4 to
5 minutes on each side, or until golden brown.

35 Calories
0.6 g Protein
9.2 g Carbohydrates
0.1 g Fat
2.6% Calories from Fat
1.3 g Fiber
0 mg Sodium
0 mg Cholesterol

GRILLED PEARS

*This versatile fruit can complement a savory serving
of pork or be served unadorned as a simple dessert.*

4 firm pears, halved, cored, and seeded

WHEN READY TO GRILL
Over medium-hot coals, place pears on a grilling grid
coated with nonstick vegetable spray. Cover grill and cook
4 to 5 minutes on each side, or until golden brown.

93 Calories
0.6 g Protein
23.8 g Carbohydrates
0.6 g Fat
5.8% Calories from Fat
4.1 g Fiber
1 mg Sodium
0 mg Cholesterol

4 SERVINGS

Grilling adds a subtle smoky flavor to this traditional accompaniment to fish or ham.

1 whole pineapple

Using a sharp knife, remove top and bottom of pineapple. With a pineapple cutter or a very sharp knife, remove outer skin and core. Slice pineapple into ½-inch slices.

WHEN READY TO GRILL
Over medium-hot coals, place pineapple slices on a grilling grid coated with nonstick vegetable spray. Cover grill and cook pineapple 4 to 6 minutes on each side, or until golden brown.

88 Calories
0.7 g Protein
21.9 g Carbohydrates
0.8 g Fat
8.2% Calories from Fat
2.1 g Fiber
2 mg Sodium
0 mg Cholesterol

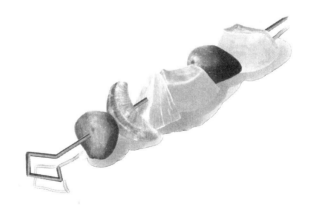

GLOSSARY

Banana peppers   Large, yellow peppers having a mild flavor.

Capers   The unopened flower bud of the caper bush that is pickled in vinegar. Used as a garnish or condiment, it adds piquancy to any dish. Found in the olive section of most supermarkets.

Chinese black beans   Fermented, salted soy beans. Found in most Asian food stores.

Chinese Five Spice powder   A mixture of cloves, cinnamon, fennel, star anise, and Szechwan peppercorns.

Cilantro   Sometimes called fresh coriander or Chinese parsley. Cilantro is a member of the parsley family. Leaves are flat and should be crisp and green. Found in Asian food stores and the produce section of most supermarkets.

Daikon (or oriental radish)   A root vegetable having a peppery taste that imparts a pungent flavor to salads. Found in Asian food stores and the produce section of most supermarkets.

Feta cheese   A soft, white Greek cheese made from goat or sheep milk and cured in salt brine. It is crumbly and has a slightly sour, salty taste.

Garam masala   An Indian spice (or curry powder) made of a combination of cardamom, cinnamon, cloves, cayenne, cumin, mace, and nutmeg. Found in most Asian food stores.

Ginger root   A rhizome or root that originated in India, but is also native to Asia. The ginger root is brown and knotty on the outside, yellow and juicy on the inside. Found in Asian food stores and the produce section of supermarkets.

Hoisin sauce   Made from fermented soybean paste, garlic, sugar, and spices. It is both sweet and spicy. Found in the Asian section of most supermarkets.

Hot bean sauce   An Asian bean sauce made from dried chile peppers or chile paste. Found in Asian food stores.

Hot Pepper Oil   A red-colored oil getting its flavor from dried chile peppers or chile paste. Used to season Szechwan dishes and found in Asian food stores and in the Asian section of most supermarkets.

Jalapeño   Green peppers that are about $1\frac{1}{2}$ to 2 inches long and 1 inch wide across the top. They are very hot.

Kalamata olives   Glossy black, almond-shaped olives, cured in red wine vinegar and packed in jars. They are frequently used in salads. Can be purchased by the pound at specialty food stores or delis.

Kecap manis   An Indonesian condiment that is a sweet soy sauce made with palm sugar. Found in Asian food stores.

Lemongrass   An herb belonging to the grass family that has a lemon-like or citrus flavor and is very aromatic. Although it can grow to be $1\frac{1}{2}$ to 2 feet long, only the bottom 6 inches is tender enough to be edible. Found in Asian food stores and in the produce section of most supermarkets.

Mirin or rice wine   A sweet cooking wine made from sake (a Japanese rice wine), rice, malt, and sweet rice. Found in Asian food stores and in the Asian section of most supermarkets.

Miso   A paste produced by salting and fermenting soybeans and rice. Used in marinades, soups, and as a meat substitute.

Oyster sauce   Made from oysters, water, and salt; imparts a salty, oyster flavor to foods. Found in Asian food stores or in the Asian section of most supermarkets.

Portobello mushrooms   Giant, cultivated mushrooms that are dark brown in color and have an open cap. Found in the produce section of most supermarkets.

Serranos   Bright green or red peppers that are about 2 inches long and $\frac{1}{4}$ inch across. The hottest of the chiles.

Sesame oil   A wonderful nutty flavored oil derived from roasted sesame seeds. Found in the Asian section of most supermarkets.

Shiitake mushrooms   Edible mushrooms frequently used in Asian dishes. They have a very rich flavor and also are high in protein. Found in Asian food stores and in the produce section of most supermarkets.

Star fruit (carambola)   A juicy and tart fruit having a smooth, waxy yellow-orange skin with five distinct ridges. When the star fruit is sliced, it resembles a star.

Szechwan chili sauce   A spicy sauce made of chile peppers, garlic, salt, and pepper. Found in Asian food stores.

Tamari   A soy sauce that is rich in taste and wheat-free.

Tandoori-style naan   A popular bread served at meals and festivals throughout India, Pakistan, and the Middle East, and is traditionally baked in a hot clay tandoori oven. Can be made into sandwiches or served as an accompaniment to a meal.

Thai curry pastes   A combination of aromatic herbs, vegetables, chiles, and spices, all ground into a paste. Yellow pastes are mild, red pastes vary in degree of heat, and green pastes are very hot. Available in Asian food stores.

Tomatillos   Mexican green tomatoes resembling cherry tomatoes, but firmer and more tart. Covered with a light green husk that is peeled away and then the resinous material covering the tomatillo is washed off before using. Found in the produce section of most supermarkets.

Vinegars:

- **Black vinegar**   An Asian vinegar that is used as a condiment.
- **Balsamic vinegar (*aceto balsamico*).**   An herbed flavored vinegar made from Italian red wine and is produced in Modena, Italy. Aged in fragrant, wooden casks for up to 70 years.
- **Red or white wine vinegar**   The color of the vinegar is determined by whether red or white wine was used.
- **Rice vinegar**   A delicately flavored Japanese vinegar.
- **Sherry vinegar**   Made from Spanish sherry.

INDEX